Harry Burger

The Null Treaties

AF145298

Harry Burger

The Null Treaties

True Story

© 2015 Harry Burger
Satz und Layout: Buch&media GmbH, München
Herstellung und Verlag: BoD – Books on Demand
Printed in Germany
ISBN 978-3-7357-0488-7

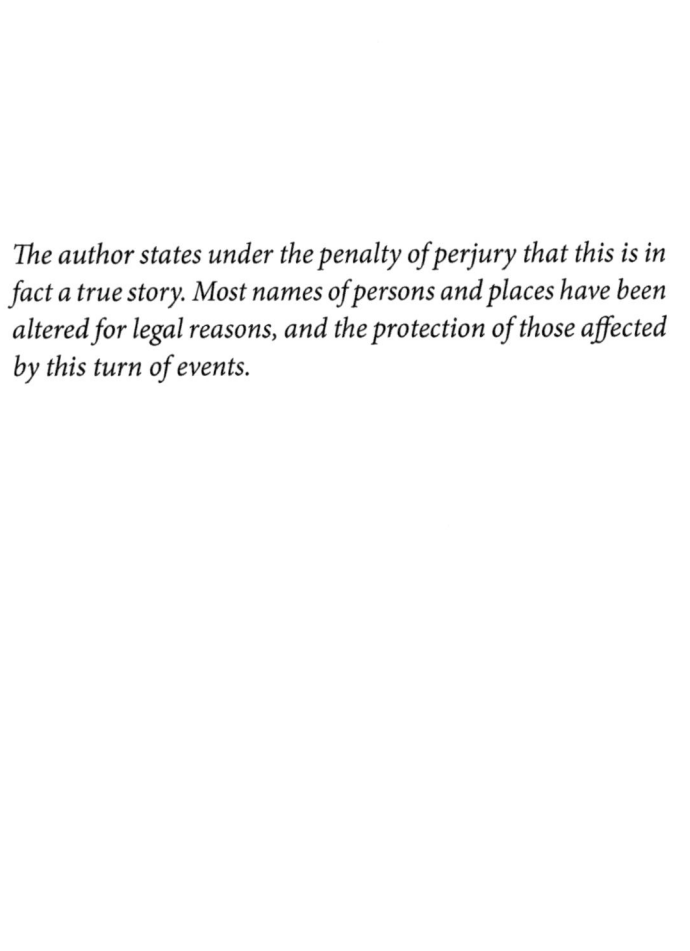

The author states under the penalty of perjury that this is in fact a true story. Most names of persons and places have been altered for legal reasons, and the protection of those affected by this turn of events.

CHAPTER ONE

After a while the monotonous humming of jet engines tends to get on one's nerves. The cramped feeling in the seats of charter airplanes are not very comfortable for tall people like me, and the lukewarm airline food leaves a lot to be desired. Nevertheless I was in a good mood. My vacations had just started. My aim was not a sandy beach under the tropical sun, or the exploration of exotic cultures and customs. Those seemed to be destinations for middle-aged people, not for a young man in his late twenties. After my mother returned very impressed from a trip through the USA a couple of years ago, I decided to visit the "New World" myself.

After hours of darkness over the Atlantic Ocean the dim lights of Bangor appeared on the horizon. The airliner took a wide curve to the left and landed smoothly on the runway of the north-eastern US City. Daybreak had barely arrived as I walked down the boarding stairs and continued towards the terminal. A dense fog began to engulf the region that late summer morning and all passengers had to wait for a couple of hours until the plane was able to start again. Restless and driven by unquenchable curiosity, I kept rubbing the steamed up windows in the terminal to catch a glimpse of the mysterious, foreign ambiance, but the town and its vicinity were too far beyond my view.

After finally reaching Chicago I rolled off a car rental company's lot, behind the steering wheel of a brand new, large station wagon. I was not fully aware of all the contracts I had just signed for taking possession of the vehicle, since my English was rather marginal at the time. To make matters more complicated a heavy downpour engulfed the south-western areas of the city, as I was still becoming accustomed with American road traffic.

My good mood remained buoyant as I was cruising along to encounter this fascinating, great world ahead of me. Soon I began to suspect that all intersections in the area seemed to have a striking similarity, until I became aware of having driven in circles for about half an hour. After close examination of the road signs, the word "West" caught my eye, and taught me that compass directions were conveniently displayed along major, American highways. Now it would have been easy to find my way, but I did not even know where I intended to travel. So I perceived the word "West" on the little sign as a recommendation. West it should be, I decided. The small country road left the huge city behind. Traffic density declined and fields, woods and farmhouses passed by my car windows as I, happy beyond one's wishes, viewed the vast American scenery for the first time in my life.

Late that afternoon the fuel gauge reminded me to stop at a gas station. The attendant realized my lack of fluency in English and offered to fill the tank with the proper type of gasoline and check the motor oil and tyre pressure. However, he refused a tip, telling me that this service was included. In appreciation of his American honesty and obligation I kindly thanked the gentleman. 'Have a good trip,' he replied as I started my engine. Some miles down the road the peaceful two-lane highway merged onto a two-way multilane freeway. The traffic was moderate, leaving me plenty of time to admire the landscape around me. Dusk was about to fall and a pinkish glow adorned a couple of little clouds on the western sky as I crossed the bridge over the Mississippi River. Night had laid its black shroud over Iowa. The hills and forests vanished from my view. Only an occasional, distant light of unknown origin interrupted the darkness surrounding me. Just the pavement in front of me was lit by my car's headlights. For inexplicable reasons I was suddenly overcome by a feeling of fear and depression. I was neither frightened by America or its people, much less by the darkness. I decided that it had to be the considerable distance from home, maybe the jet lag, or perhaps the lack of sleep during the last day, so I thought. I am not superstitious, but looking back it could have been a hint of my subconscious mind. Something might have tried to warn me, not to pursue my path any further, but I kept on driving, westward towards my destiny.

I arrived at the city of Des Moines. Tired as can be I found a motel room on the outskirts of town. As I woke up the next day the sun was already standing high in the sky. After an extensive, hot shower I stepped outside, where a beautiful, bright day was awaiting me. The motel owner asked me if I had slept well. I smiled; this question might have been intended ironically, since it was almost noon. Slowly I backed the car out of the parking space. Once more I received a jovial 'have a nice trip,' before I turned onto the access road to the freeway. My despondent feeling from last night was gone and I was eager to continue my exploration of America.

The colours of the landscape changed gradually from profound green to brownish yellow. The horizon seemed to move farther away beyond the flat landscape of the Midwest. And the sky appeared wide and mighty, stretching its blue yonder over the tremendous size of this big country. I kept asking myself how it must feel to live in a place as huge as this. Nebraska's endless cornfields were lining the freeway on its course to the adorable mountain lands of Wyoming. I just kept on rolling, restless as if I was afraid to miss something worth seeing further ahead. Driving through the awesome deserts of Utah and Nevada was indeed another astounding experience.

After a comfortable night's rest in a motel my dependable rental car bravely climbed up the Sierra Nevada, where I was received by an enchanting alpine paradise. I had left the freeway and continued on the curvy two-lane road following the shores of Lake Tahoe. The fir tree covered mountain peaks threw their tranquil reflections over the calm surface of the clear water. A scent of mountain pine lay in the air. The quiet beauty of this area remained largely undisturbed. Only occasionally would a powerboat or a car passing by on the road interrupt the idyll.

My voyage finally brought me to the pacific coast. I was now south of Los Angeles, where I parked in a quiet, open area by the sea. Silently, almost in a state of rapt devotion, I kept gazing at the largest ocean in the world. After half a day in this region I realized that I was breathing easier, less afflicted by asthma and other chronic allergies that had dogged me since childhood. I realized that this arid climate near the sea was very favourable to my health. For that reason in particular, I would have enjoyed remaining for a few additional days in south-western California, but with a two thousand mile return trip ahead of me, it seemed prudent not to waste time.

With a touch of melancholy in my heart I kept glancing in the rear view mirror on my journey back to the Midwest, and a feeling of sadness came over me as I boarded the airplane. I did not want to depart from this country so soon. America had left a deep and lasting impression upon me and an inevitable desire to return.

After returning to my home country I developed an increasing curiosity and fascination about the USA and everything American. Back in those days the Vietnam War evoked widespread criticism of America within Europe. It almost seemed as if we Europeans had forgotten that America helped liberate us from Nazi oppression, and that they had subsequently established their military bases in our continent to keep the communist eastern block off our backs. Europe's prosperity, the rights, freedom and security of its population were therefore, in part, America's credit, and the American soldiers who fell in Europe during the Second World War deserved our respect and gratitude. Enhanced by my short, but impressive visit in the New World my pro-Americanism flourished to new heights, right along with my affection for that country.

One day I glanced at the Arizona license plates of an automobile, parked nearby my European home. I spotted a gentleman taking pictures with his camera. 'Good afternoon sir,' I started the conversation, 'Are you from Arizona?'

'Good afternoon,' he replied, 'No, my wife and I live in San Alberto, California. We just bought the car in Arizona.'

'Isn't that a coincidence,' I returned, "I just passed by your hometown a few months ago!"

Meanwhile my mother joined in on the conversation, 'Please come on in; would you like a cup of coffee?' Later that day we invited our American guests for supper. Phil and Dora Emerson became my first American acquaintances and I could hardly wait to visit them in California next year.

I felt at home as I drove down the US east coast the following summer. This time I had chosen the southern route to California, where I met Phil and Dora again. I was almost embarrassed over the warm welcome and hospitality I received upon my unannounced arrival. After I expressed my interest to immigrate to the USA in the future, the friendly couple seemed eager to become my immigration sponsors.

The subsequent day I travelled with Phil to San Francisco to meet Paul Stoller, his son in law. Again, I was cordially invited into an American home like a member of the family by people I barely even knew. A couple of days later I rolled across the country again from its south-western border all the way to north-eastern Maine. I talked to Americans from almost every walk of life; I looked around, observed, and gathered information. I only came upon interesting experiences. Nothing I saw or heard left a negative impression upon me. Yet, it was always around me, the dark side of America, which I never saw, because it was hidden where I least expected it.

After having found a region where I could live without chronic allergies, I decided to inquire about options regarding my immigration to the United States of America. 'I am sorry to tell you that Americans may only sponsor family members for immigration into our country,' the US Consul responded to my enquiry. 'Under the old laws, US citizens were permitted to sponsor any foreigner to come to America, but the rules have changed. Nowadays only certain professionals, family members of US citizens and those of lawful residents in the USA are readily admitted for immigration.'

'In other words it has become nearly impossible for average Europeans to live and work in America?' I replied.

'No, I would not say that, it has just become more difficult,' the diplomat answered politely. 'Nothing is impossible!' he added with a broad smile.

CHAPTER TWO

To cope with the death of one's mother may be the most difficult moment in a man's life. It was around Easter, when my mom lost her battle with cancer. Her life had not been a bed of roses, but she was always there for me as a little child in need of love and comfort. She was there for me as an adolescent seeking guidance, and as a teacher and friend in my early adulthood. So this was her last goodbye. I sold our family home and quit my job. I just felt like taking a break for a while. And the most suitable place for doing that seemed obvious to me. Once more the big silver bird lifted off the runway, heading westward as always, to the land of my dreams. But the term "Nightmare" would have been a mild understatement for what America had in store for me this time.

The climatic wonderland of coastal southern California was awaiting me with sunshine, pleasant temperatures, endless sandy beaches and its soothing air from the Pacific Ocean. My tourist visa was valid for an entire year. This was plenty of time to relax for a while and continue my immigration efforts. I worked on my English, got to know my way around San Alberto and learned about customs and daily life in America. I became acquainted with Americans and began to read American newspapers and magazines. Occasionally I relaxed at the beach and went for a swim in the ocean. Still I could not always interpret the menu selection in restaurants. After the waitress brought the food, accompanied by the friendly words 'enjoy you meal,' I felt tempted to say, 'that's not what I ordered,' but obviously I did. Also the occasional reply 'I am sorry, I did not get that,' was an indicator that my English needed improving. Years of training lay ahead of me to achieve fluency in this language.

Meanwhile a few months had passed since my latest arrival in the country and it was time to examine my options for immigration into America. Accompanied by Phil Emerson I visited the regional office of the US Immigration and Naturalization Service in San Alberto. Together with Paul Stoller I consulted a lawyer specialized in immigration matters in San Francisco. Thereafter I sought advice from an attorney in San Alberto, but the answers were always the same: 'Sorry, but no.' Meanwhile my American friends provided me with a little official folder from the US Government, containing all the rules and regulations for foreigners to immigrate into the USA. Its contents were discouraging. Only certain skilled professionals, refugees from communist nations, close relatives of US citizens and very close relatives of lawful immigrants were admitted for permanent residency in this nation.

Among my circle of American friends was John Sullivan, a sales manager of a sizeable, regional company selling transportation equipment like trucks, trailers, forklifts and the like. The born and raised Anglo American was a friendly, jovial gentleman in his late thirties, stocky, with a bushy moustache and receding hairline. He seemed always in the mood for a spontaneous, ironic remark, or a joke and a good laugh, which was rather untypical for most US Americans I had met so far. John accompanied me to one more meeting with an attorney. We were told that not even a waiting list for prospective immigrants existed, and my chances for being granted an immigration permit to America were basically zero.

'Why don't you find yourself an American wife,' John said 'you will get an immigrant green card right away and US citizenship three years later?' was his simple recipe for my problem. However I'd had a recent conversation with an American lady who married a Latin American immigrant not long ago and her matrimony was subjected to undue scrutiny with her husband being arbitrarily deported from the country. In the face of restrictive immigration laws, the federal government appeared very eager to deport anybody suspected of living here illegally. For these reasons, a quickly arranged marriage did not appear to be an option for me.

My American Dream seemed to be terminating in a cul-de-sac. Obviously it was time for me to pack my bags and make provisions for my departure. But I'd noticed that improvements to my health were quite significant during the past half year in coastal southern California, which made me even more reluctant to accept a no for an answer regarding my desire to live in this country.

The rainy season had set in. The sky was often cloudy in this area, a place usually spoiled by sunshine most of the year. But wintertime in San Alberto had a charm of its own; principally marked by mild temperatures that rarely fell to freezing point at night. The weather in this arid region appeared relatively calm all year round. Thunderstorms were rare and hail and snow were practically unknown. Protected by two bays, the city of San Alberto extends right to the waterfront with its centre barely one hundred feet above sea level. The mostly flat, sandy beaches of San Alberto County ascend moderately into the hillsides of the adjoining landscape, leaving ample space for sports and leisure by the sea. Further inland, the grounds become more rugged and often divided by little canyons. Although the surroundings appear rather bare compared to the lush, green vegetation of Western Europe, I perceived coastal Southern California as a wonderful place to be.

It was within the first months of the New Year when I responded to a TV commercial of a nationwide group of immigration attorneys, and asked for an appointment. I was expecting another one of those 'we are so sorry but we are unable to help you,' replies, but I was in for a delightful surprise. 'You may not be able to immigrate into the USA at this time or in the foreseeable future,' the lawyer's assistant advised me, 'but in order to live here, an actual immigration is not always necessary. Just about every Western European Nation, as well as innumerable countries around the entire world maintains friendship, commerce, and extradition conventions with the USA. These treaties entitle citizens from these commonwealths to establish themselves here, and US citizens to live in those cosignatory states. Principal immigration laws are unaffected by these provisos.

'Aliens admitted in nations under these reciprocal agreements must not be subjected to any condition whatsoever to which a citizen of the country where they reside shall not be subjected. The only two exceptions being political rights and participation in the properties of communities, corporations or institutions explicitly reserved for citizens of that country.'

After listening silently to this new information and reading some of the accompanying text presented to me, the legal assistant showed me an excerpt from the US Constitution: *Treaties are the Supreme Law of the Land.* 'However,' she added, 'an investment within the USA is required to qualify under this proviso. Previously the minimum amount necessary was forty thousand dollars; nowadays one hundred thousand dollars is about the bottom line.'

What I just heard had really made my day. After this heartening legal advice I needed some business advice as well. The first whom I informed about the good news was John Sullivan. He agreed to accompany me to the lawyer's office the subsequent day. Most of the lawyer's eloquent explanations went clearly over my head, so I attended the meeting as a silent listener. John gave me a briefing afterwards.

'The way I understand this treaty arrangement, it does not seem that a foreigner may merely acquire tools to make a living over here, or place his funds into a bank account. Investments must be made into an ongoing bona fide enterprise, preferably providing employment for US citizens. After those investments have been made into an existing business or the foundation of a new enterprise, the application for a treaty investor visa may be presented to our government for approval. Within this timeframe of approximately three months the applicant must remain in the USA and is not permitted to leave and re-enter the country.' Somewhat confused by John's recount of the meeting, I asked, 'But my permit to live here will be issued, right?' 'According to the lawyer; yes!' I have always been a cautious man by nature. There was no reason for me to doubt the attorney's words. Additionally, I felt more comfortable having all this information confirmed by qualified, backed up opinions. The results were positive; two lawyers attested the validity of the convention at issue and all stipulations and particulars thereof as stated. I was also assured full protection by the US Constitution, including the bill of rights and its amendment XIV, guaranteeing civil rights to the population of this country, citizens and noncitizens alike.

'There are always plenty of opportunities in this country,' John assured me. 'From what you have told me you have many years of experience in the armoured car, as well as the transportation trade. If you are contemplating, as you have indicated to me, to set up a freight forwarding business in the area, then you can definitely count on my help. The most crucial aspect is to start an enterprise from scratch, but I have plenty of business connections in every aspect of commerce surrounding this line of work.'

The following week, John and I travelled to San Francisco where we obtained professional advice from Paul Stoller. He was after all a renowned certified public accountant, tax specialist and lecturer at a university. 'I'm glad you've found a way to stay in America!' Paul greeted me cordially. 'I always anticipated that there must be a provision for you to establish yourself here.' Paul's professional input was essential for my starting up a company in California. Once more I had to be a bystander to the discussions and leave the subject up to John. I was making progress in my English, but I was not yet ready for all the technical jargon surrounding tax regulations and business law.

Paul accepted my offer to become an honorary member on the board of directors in my company. I needed competent people on my side and in my business in order to be successful and Paul's input was very essential. All details of my new American livelihood needed to be well conceived, and every aspect well covered. Being protected under this treaty gave me additional confidence that my future as a treaty investor in the United States would be built upon rock solid grounds. My American future began to materialize at last. My faith in the United States of America was unbroken. After an entire year in this country I had not yet sensed the remotest indication to doubt this Nation's hallmark status as a place of impeccable integrity and undeniable justice and equality. And I was about to become a patriot of my new, chosen homeland.

I needed to inform my home country regarding my taking up residency in the USA. John accompanied me on my trip to Los Angeles. 'Do you like it here?' the consular secretary asked me politely as he typed my name on a document. 'Yes Sir,' I replied adamantly, 'the climate here is very favourable to my health.'

'You're not the first who has told me so. It is indeed very pleasant in this region. – All right, now we have you registered here with us.' He said as he turned back to my direction. 'I have an E – Visa application pending Sir, as a treaty investor, I am starting a business over here,' I explained.

'Oh, we are not concerned about the visas of our people,

we only like to know where they are within the US,' the secretary answered politely. I did not receive any further comments from the diplomat, no recommendations or much less an unambiguous warning, which should have been mandatory under the circumstances.

Based upon John and Paul's recommendation, my American business became a corporation. I had already acquired equipment and signed a rental contract for an office in Escondera, a north-eastern suburb of San Alberto. After my change of status from a visitor to a resident and entrepreneur in the USA, I became aware of remarkable distinctions between the New World and the country where I was born and raised. Most notable were begging letters arriving at our office. These were not drawn up by charity organizations, but by law enforcement associations from various US States. Their monetary demands ranged from three to four digit amounts.

Fred, the operations manager of my business, a born and raised US Citizen in his mid thirties with many years experience in the trade, seemed pretty much at a loss to answer my questions regarding this practice. In Europe I had never heard about the police collecting funds from businesses or private individuals. John's office at the equipment dealership was fortunately just across the parking lot; so that's where I went, somewhat perturbed, with this correspondence. 'I simply would throw away that kind of bogus,' was John's answer. 'The term law enforcement is clearly defined from a literary aspect, but not necessarily reserved by law for exclusive use by government. Almost everybody may use these words for himself. As a matter of fact, our government agencies are terribly embarrassed over these schemes.'

'So this is undoubtedly the work of impostures and in no way connected with any public officials?' John's expression became pensive as I awaited his reply. 'I wish I could give you a definitive answer, but I can't. There is always a remote possibility that some black sheep in our system are participating in these types of activities.'

'Why isn't the government doing anything about it?' I asked surprised.

'They do, but the perpetrators must be apprehended, charged and convicted. Most crooks over here are shrewd and quick in circumventing the laws.'

Only a couple of weeks later Fred advised me about an unusual visitor who came to our office during my absence. The gentleman allegedly claimed to be a plain-clothes officer from a police department in Escondera where our office was located. According to Fred he was asking for a one hundred dollar donation to the police. When I was told that this request had not been met, I felt the hair on my neck beginning to stand up. This time I arrived right out frightened at John's office. 'I am getting confronted with peculiar actions from officials, and I don't know how to react!'

'Just don't get upset,' John replied, 'It is customary in many US regions for businesses selling merchandise or offering services within a town, to make an annual contribution to the local police.'

'So Fred omitted paying protection money to the constables?' A smile came over John's face as he responded, 'For goodness sake, no, we are not a banana republic and you are not a local merchant but an interstate freight forwarder.

You are not obligated to pay such contributions.' John's explanation was convincing, his experience in the realm of US commerce was considerable, and his self-confidence almost contagious. I was merely a kind of apprentice in American business. Yet the dimensions of this nation are huge and the probable complexity of its system so vast, that an entire human lifetime would be insufficient to comprehend all of its intricacies.

I was contemplating carrying one hundred dollars to the police station on my own, but I did not know the name of the money collector who apparently visited our office. To fumble around with big bank bills in a police station seemed like the proverbial sword with two edges. If the alleged policeman was in fact an imposture, then I would look like I was bribing a constable. It was a situation referred to as being between a rock and a hard place. Eventually I told Fred to hand over a one hundred dollar check, made out to the Escondera Police Department, if that gentleman should come back. Despite John's calming words, I had an uneasy feeling about this strange encounter, and hoped it had no further consequences.

John realized that I was becoming concerned about some obviously customary procedures in America that I had recently come in contact with. 'Let's go down to the superior court in San Alberto,' he told me spontaneously. 'I want to show you how our system works.' In the subsequent hours we watched a number of court proceedings.

'Virtually anybody in this country, believing having been subjected to wrongdoing may come here. This place is obligated to make any wrongs right again, by the powers of the law and it does so absolutely impartially and objectively. This is an essential part of what makes this country great. We make mistakes over here, as happens everywhere in the world. We also have our share of wickedness being committed in our society, but we are a democratic state of rights. You are experiencing some cultural shock over the differences between our approach to justice and liberty compared to prevailing procedures in your home country.'

John appeared to be a patriot, but he was by no means uncritical or gullible. 'We are not always perfect over here, but relentlessly striving to be. Just give it some time, until you get completely acquainted with our environment.' He was probably right. I needed to adjust and to accept the characteristics of my chosen home country, without overreacting to every peculiarity I came across. 'You have exactly the same rights as everybody else in this country, except you are not yet eligible to vote.' Johns reassuring words seemed comforting and convincing. It was obviously up to me to develop more faith in the US system.

Around that time I became associated with Louis Martin. He was an experienced insurance businessman in his forties. The stocky, energetic Anglo-American seemed the ideal business partner for my intentions to diversify my little enterprise. I planned to start an insurance venture predominately catering to the transportation industry. In the meantime, I had decided to offer stock options in my corporation to our staff including John Sullivan, Fred Steiger, our lead driver Dan Health, as well as our close associates Louis Martin and Paul Stoller. I offered these in conjunction with additional incentives to encourage optimal performance and loyalty on the part of our key personnel. So it was no longer my company, but ours.

CHAPTER THREE

In the coming fall John advised me of a remarkable opportunity. A transportation business apparently beset by administrative problems was contemplating handing over their late model trucks to owner/operators within an ongoing freight forwarding company. Our corporation had expanded its clientele rapidly and plenty of work was available for those refrigerated semi-trucks. The challenge of this venture that faced us now was the additional capital required to cover the operation costs until our bills were issued and paid by the customers. John had invested a lot of time analysing all the particulars of this engagement; our attorney was contacted accordingly and meetings were held to discuss these issues in every aspect. The proposed contract looked as safe and sound as can be. Nonetheless, I was still reluctant on account of the fact that this deal required not only all my personal assets, but also a six-digit loan from a friend in Europe.

'I understand your hesitancy,' John said empathically, 'but I did not mean to tell you this right away, since I did not want to alarm you; your visa application has been denied. Your investment of $ 150,000 was deemed to be insufficient, but your attorney seems very confident that the proposed, additional investments for this venture would satisfy our government and your treaty investor status will be approved.' I glanced at John for a moment, before gazing pensively at the surface of the desk ahead of me. 'I suppose it's down to "in for a penny, in for a pound,"' was my short reply to this alarming news. Those, at best, vaguely defined investment requirements in order to be granted admission in this nation, were additional aspects to wonder about in regard to American rules and regulations. I remembered my determination to have faith in America. – When in Rome do as the Romans do.

'This was my primary reason to consider this prospective business deal,' John continued in reply to my silence. I sensed being trapped, with the only possible path heading forward.

I was working in our office on a daily basis, sometimes including weekends to overview our expanding operation. In light of the additional commercial vehicles, developing ventures in insurance, and plans to engage in public relations and import/export activities, we had acquired a business computer system. In those days computer software was not sold in every department store. In particular a commercial computer needed extensive setting up and programming by a qualified specialist for a couple of months, until it was ready for operation. We hired Don Bricklin for this task, who also assisted us in making the right choice regarding this purchase. Don was a knowledgeable computer expert from the immediate region and, according to our inquiries, well qualified to do the job.

I had signed the contract to integrate this fleet of trucks into our dispatch system and finally provided the funds necessary for doing so. Unfortunately, after the first of these units arrived at our facility, it was apparent that they were not in perfect operating condition as agreed. Some vehicles were in need of extensive maintenance.

Gradually we succeeded in repairing all these trucks to satisfactory order for prospective owner/operators ready to work for us. Gale Cassell, former manager of this troubled fleet of vehicles, was a stocky, heavy set and well-mannered Anglo-American in his early fifties. He seemed relieved about turning over his operation, but appeared to have problems parting with his company, as he kept hanging around in our office. He also seemed to be dissatisfied with about every prospective owner/operator we were able to summon for taking over these vehicles.

'He's getting into his years,' was John's assessment of the situation. 'Cassell and his bean counting associates ran that business into the ground, but he still thinks of himself as indispensable. Just give him another week or two and we will have seen the last of him.'

'Initially he appeared to be forthcoming and polite, but he is getting increasingly pushy, and interfering with our day to day operation.'

Gale Cassell had still not disappeared a month later. I became annoyed over his fraternizing with some of our personnel, and held a private conversation with Fred regarding this matter. Fred was as tired of having Cassell around the office as I was, but he never saw any indications of suspicious conduct on Cassell's part. It was in the following days that I became aware that company records were disappearing and immediately informed John. At the time, John was still working as a manager of the nearby equipment dealership and supervised our corporation on a part time basis. At the same time, charges to our credit accounts had suddenly jumped to soaring heights. Right away I informed all businesses delivering goods or services to our company to stop all non-cash orders. I also requested a list of any charges made to our accounts during the last three-months.

How Cassell and his co-accessories obviously managed to convert uncounted incoming payments destined for our corporation remains a mystery to this date. As I tried to piece this puzzle together it became increasingly evident that a group of individuals surrounding Gale Cassell had apparently succeeded to cause losses and damages amounting to six digit figures to our company within only a quarter of a year. Since these individuals were not only converting innumerable incoming payments, but also abolishing every record pertaining to those, we had unfortunately become aware of these crafty schemes too late and were unable to react in time. They had also been successful in intercepting some of our incoming mail, containing the status of our company accounts. By those means they obviously managed to make fraudulent charges until these accounts were overdrawn.

'Oh Jesus Christ!' John shouted helplessly, 'This is my entire damned fault. I haven't been watching these people. I've already made an appointment with our corporate attorney in one hour. Secondly, I've just hired an auditing business. Two gentlemen are due here within the next half hour. Nobody must interfere with their work and nobody is to give them any orders, please. They will gather all records anywhere within our facility.' John turned to me. 'You must call Paul Stoller. He needs to come down here on the double. I'll be taking a leave of absence from my place of employment in the equipment dealership. I am responsible for what happened here, so it is my obligation to clean up this mess. This is my life principle. You should stay here and wait for the auditing people. Fred, are all remaining vehicles under our control?'

'I suppose so,' Fred answered.

'I'm on my way to the lawyer's office,' John continued, 'When I come back the two of us must go to the police and file charges! By the way has anybody seen Gale Cassell?' Fred and I shook our heads. 'That's what I suspected,' John replied.

Louis Martin stepped into the office about ten minutes later. "What is going on here?" he'd noticed our earnest expressions. 'We're under siege,' I answered. 'Gale Cassell appears to be part of an organized white collar crime organization.' Louis appeared astounded as he shook his head. "Where's John?'

'He went to San Alberto to see the lawyer,' I replied. I started to compile an inventory list based upon some remaining records and handed it to the two gentlemen from the auditing firm as they arrived. Meanwhile, John returned from the lawyer's office. 'What did the attorney say?' I wanted to know.

'Not much, we need to prepare a list of stolen inventory; I need to file charges at the District Attorney's Office tomorrow.'

'How about going to the police?' I asked.

'What we can prove at this time is grand fraud, contractual breach, embezzlement, theft and conversion. The District Attorney has jurisdiction over these offenses, not the police.'

'Where are Don Bricklin and Dan Health?' John wanted to know, but all of us were at a loss as to the whereabouts of our computer specialist and lead driver. 'Damned!' John muttered.

'The signatures of the two guys you've just mentioned show up on uncounted unauthorized purchases charged to our accounts,' I added.

'Have you checked our computer system?" John asked as he hurried to the computer.

'No I don't think anybody did,' I returned.

'That's exactly what I expected,' John concluded as he started the computer and checked the drawers for the diskettes.

'Somebody took all the data, and erased the entire programming,' John sighed deeply. 'I'll take the computer home tonight, and try to reload it with what I've got at home,' he glanced in my direction. I could sense the tension and I was also considerably concerned. 'Yes of course,' I said after a short moment of silence, in light of all the confusion going on. Our next surprise was awaiting us when we came back the following morning. We obviously had some unannounced visitors during the past night. In summary it was almost easier to establish what had been left, than what had been taken. Some of our desks were pried open and most of the records, including those neatly gathered and sorted out by the auditing company were gone. Our shop behind the office had also been looted and our little petty cash box was empty. 'Now this was a burglary, let's go to the police,' John said with a trembling voice. 'How many vehicles are missing?' he continued in my direction. I made a quick inventory of the vehicles, 'Five, it appears.' I couldn't believe I was on the receiving end of these acts that were being played out and it bore a horrible feeling in my gut. Surely it was just a matter of going through the legal process and this whole, ridiculous ordeal would be sorted out.

At the police station the two of us were led to the office of a couple of plain-clothes officers with a rather morose expression on their faces. The two constables were broad shouldered, white Americans around forty years old. One of them was rather tall, the other stocky. John informed them about the burglary in our office the previous night and also mentioned the group of people around Gale Cassell as likely suspects. He received a very frosty reply from the tall officer. 'From what you are telling us this seems to be a civil issue. These types of disputes do not fall under the purview of the police.'

As I glanced at the two policemen for a moment, I became aware that the stocky constable was glowering at me as if I were some kind of monster. I couldn't place his face and I was certain that I'd had no encounters with him. I finally put down his attitude to him having a bad day and we were just another aspect of that. After all, my improprieties committed in this country amounted to a mere parking ticked I got in San Francisco over a year ago. But on the way back to the office I recalled our omission to pay a financial contribution to this police department. Was this a crucial mistake coming back to haunt us now? Additionally, we were both concerned about the lack of response we were just confronted with.

At my request, most of our business connections sent us copies of transaction records as I requested. I came upon my own forged signatures a number of times ordering purchases I'd never authorized, and names of businesses I'd never heard of. But worst of all – these fraudulent charges were still being made as I sat there at my desk, and those types of bills still kept coming in! When John got back from the D.A.'s office, I did not want to ask what he might have accomplished, but I must have kept looking at him as if I was expecting a statement. 'I did not get much cooperation at the district attorney's offices,' he said. 'It also appears that Cassell has filed a suit against us.'

'What...?' I shouted in disbelief.

'You heard me,' John returned.

'What is he trying to sue us for?'

'Oh, just about everything he and his cronies are committing against us!'

'This is totally unreal, it's insane!' I shook my head in disbelief.

'It is, but I have to keep a clear head, we are obviously not dealing with chicken thieves. By the way, have you called Stoller?'

'Yes he is due in the day after tomorrow.'

John got up, 'I need to talk to our suppliers. And the locksmith should be here in about half an hour. We should have changed our locks right away, but that slipped my mind amidst all the commotion. Dan Health still has a key to our facility.'

After I picked up Paul and his associate at the airport, we quickly started a conversation about the current problems in our company. Paul was asking a lot of questions, which I answered as precisely as I could. 'Meanwhile, we have so many records missing that it is difficult to assess all the damages. And there are still fraudulent charges incurred to our business as we are talking to each other right now,' I stressed. But Paul appeared rather calm, if not to say unchallenged, by the situation. He showed little – if any – interest in stopping or prosecuting the perpetrators. I almost got the impression that he was trying to convince me that, for instance, a painter obviously paints, a shoemaker would logically make shoes, and a crook will consequently commit fraud. I just could not follow this type of corkscrew logic. At the time, it seemed to me to be some kind of American approach, and Paul was not a criminologist but a CPA, primarily interested in profits or losses, regardless of their origin. Paul and I had always enjoyed conversations in a very relaxed and friendly atmosphere in the past. Now he replied in an almost cold and legalistic tone of voice. He also concluded that a six-digit amount of money had been lost, without making any comments on how it happened or who the perpetrators were. Late that afternoon he asked me to visit him at the hotel where he stayed, since he needed to talk to me. I could not see any reason to discuss anything thirty miles away, which could be said right there and then, but I complied with his request all the same.

After my arrival Paul informed me that considerable amounts of money had passed through John Sullivan's hands. This was not news to me, and I told Paul that the cash turnover in our line of commerce was very high. He acknowledged my explanation without any comment, almost as if he didn't want to hear it. Then he showed me a couple of reimbursement checks. John had forgotten to mark those properly. So I explained the circumstance. In summary I was irritated over our CPA wasting time on trivial issues, as a group of criminals were still defrauding our business.

Dusk had fallen over San Alberto as I left the hotel building and stepped outside into the mild springtime air of a southern California evening. The crowns of the majestic palm trees lining the driveway were beautifully lit by coloured spotlights and crickets were chirping in the adjoining grasslands. I slowly walked towards my car, opened the door and sat down. There I pensively remained for about ten minutes, and I could not help thinking that I might have misjudged another American associate of mine.

The following day Paul gathered most of our remaining business records to establish an audit. John and I were awaiting the results in eager anticipation. In the following weeks the mailman brought us a meagre, little wrapper from Paul's office. Its contents consisted of Paul's resignation letter from our company's board of directors, and a couple of filled out tax forms. 'Can you believe this?' John shouted, 'Your friend Stoller is trying to pass on Cassell's tax liabilities to our corporation!' I sighed deeply.

I was trying to get a handle on the deceit happening around me. I answered in a single word, 'Yes.' After John and I kept looking at each other in silence, I resumed our short conversation. 'I suppose I ought to call this gentleman.' So I dialled Paul's phone number. 'Hello Paul, how are you?'

'I'm fine,' he answered, 'how about you?'

'Could be better,' I returned, 'I just wanted to know about the status of our audit.'

'Hasn't it arrived at your place yet? I sent it off to you a couple of days ago.'

'All I got from you are a couple of tax forms, and you resignation letter.'

'Yes, that's what I mean; it is all you really need.'

'I'm sorry Paul, we were expecting an audit. To establish our tax liabilities we sent you the necessary records!'

'Well, you know, an audit would cost you about seven thousand dollars and, in light of the circumstances, I would not recommend this expenditure to you, particularly in your business's current financial situation. I got a lot of work to do right now, so if you have any other questions contact me again, have a nice day.'

'Stoller?' John seemed to be in disbelief, as he kept looking at me still holding the phone earpiece over my head after the conversation was already over for half a minute. 'Yes, Stoller…!' I returned, as I took a deep breath. 'He could have been the one who sent the Cassell Group down here to us initially, to use us as a patsy' I continued. 'Its lunchtime, lets go and get a bite to eat,' John suggested. As we sat down in the restaurant, John resumed the conversation.

'I had every angle covered in this business relationship. As you know our attorney co-signed this contract, which was approved by the US Bankruptcy Court, since Cassell's company had filed for subchapter 11 creditor's protection. But,' John said with an almost guilty undertone, 'I was not prepared for the mafia!'

'Who are these people?' I wanted to know.

'It all appears like some underworld group. A number of CPAs offering tax shelters to their clients in the form of investments in commercial vehicles. Those investments are deductible from income taxes and are therefore a popular instrument to reduce the fiscal burden for people with a relatively high income. And Gale Cassell operated his transportation business with these trucks,' John explained.

'Is that absolutely legal?' I wondered.

'Perfectly legitimate, but I am also getting hints from parts of the business community, that Cassell might be involved in large scale offshore money laundering, and his transportation business appears to be some sham operation connected therewith.'

'How about this suit Cassell filed against us?'

'That was just some type of alibi, as far as I see it. The lawyer that helped him in doing so had advised me he wanted nothing to do with Cassell and his associates anymore. Cassell is obviously convincing his creditors as well as government agencies that we are the criminals, not him and his stooges. Now, from the looks of it, he seems to have Stoller on his side.' I couldn't believe that Stoller, whom was one of the first people I'd befriended on arriving in the US and as the son in law of those friendly tourists I'd first encountered in Europe, had turned like this.

'Where do Health and Bricklin fit into this picture?' I asked. 'Bricklin had access to our data when installing our computer. Cassell must have offered Bricklin a reward to deprive us of those records, since those could have been used to prove fraud, theft and conversion by Cassell and his people committed against us. Health was on our board of directors, he knew where we kept all the written records and he apparently deprived us of those. But what these people did not know was, that I kept copies of most relevant documentation pertinent to our business operations at home, in the form of paper as well as computer data. Now I am piecing everything together to reconstruct this entire trail of intrigue.'

'Where's Louis, I haven't seen him for days?'

John checked his watch, 'He's working on a sizeable business deal for us. We've established numerous connections with Mexican Freight Carriers to handle their import and export shipments of freight from and to the south-western US Borders.'

I was unsure about this, considering our unforeseen sudden shortage in vehicles, 'Do we have enough vehicles to handle it?'

'Not at this moment, but I have some additional units lined up and one of our missing trucks is on its way back from Texas and our small truck has been found in northern California.'

'Is our computer system working again?' I wanted to know.

'Almost,' John replied. 'I've got a new programmer helping me. We need that instrument for the bookkeeping; the paperwork involved with our new Mexican Partners is very extensive. And by the way, I put a little booklet on your desk. It contains our US Constitution; so you'll know about your rights in this country.'

When we returned to the office, Fred was all shook up. 'Our phones are down!' he said. John quickly went to the next payphone nearby. 'The Cassell group keeps charging third party billings to our numbers, our phone bill is astronomical!' He informed us after he came back. 'Now I have to go and see what I can do at the phone company,' John concluded. 'Every time I put out a fire set by those individuals, they start a new one somewhere else!' he shouted angrily as he left the office. I sat at my desk, studying the US-Constitutional Amendment XIV in the little booklet in front of me.

No State (of the USA) *shall make or enforce any law which shall abridge the privileges or immunities of citizens of the United States; nor shall any State deprive any person of life, liberty, or property, without due process of law; nor deny to any person within its jurisdiction the equal protection of the laws.*

I recognized that my civil rights were constitutionally guaranteed, although the current turn of events did not really seem to support these solemn words. 'Are the phones back on?' John wanted to know as he stepped back in. 'Yes,' Fred confirmed.

'As you both must have noticed, I had to lay off some personnel,' John continued. 'I am also working on a resolution with our insurance carrier respective to all the items stolen from our facility, but I need police reports confirming the burglaries. I am on my way to the police now.' John was in and out all day long those days. At night he often worked on the computer. His family was facing some real shortcomings from the side of their dad and husband.

The disappointed look on his face when he returned from the police headquarters made further explanations unnecessary. 'I am just not getting any cooperation from the police,' was his brief statement. It was a very disconcerting experience, particularly in the precarious financial situation we found ourselves in. I had decided to talk to our corporate legal counsel alone and in person to discuss the complex issue, despite my articulacy in the English language still being only moderate. I was being met with attention and concern, but without any precise recommendation to resolve the problem.

America showed me its peculiarities and John was beginning to realize that theory and practice of US law could be different issues indeed. Amidst all this turmoil, the creditor from my homeland announced his visit, and I spent sleepless nights over our inability to pay him the interest due on his loan. However, the gentleman demonstrated generous understanding of our difficulties and the meeting concluded in a cordial, friendly atmosphere.

Relieved by this outcome at least, I entered our office the subsequent Monday morning. A glance through our facility took my breath away. The very desk reserved for our computer system was completely empty. The system could have been at John's residence, but innumerable supplies for the instrument remained in the office. Fred and our secretary seemed to sit unsuspecting at their desks, as I, without saying a word, walked over to the second entrance of our facility. This door was always locked, including during business hours, but as I carefully pushed against it with my hip it gave way. Now I saw the remains of the lock cylinder in the form of crumbs and burrs lying outside. I asked our personnel to stay clear of the office, not to enter our shop, and not to touch door-knobs. Then I realized that the alarm system I had installed was recently disabled. I did not feel like wasting time on the telephone and rushed to John's house, where I rung the bell insistently.

'Our office was broken into; our entire computer system is missing.' John's wife, perplexed over my unfriendly announcement, met me at the door. 'Oh, my goodness, our house door,' she replied. 'I told my husband I was really sure that I had locked the house when we went out last night!'

'Oh shit!' an expression not usually in my vocabulary slipped my mouth. – A provoked reaction in the face of such circumstances.

John appeared in a bathrobe, his face was pale as linen. 'I did not realize the burglary here last night when we came home, it was very late,' he said with an expression as if he had seen a ghost.

'Did they get everything?' was my next question.

'Absolutely everything is gone.' John said with a trembling voice. After taking a deep breath I asked, 'Are you going to call the police?'

'Yes we will,' John's wife replied, on behalf of her husband who remained silently in shock.

On my way back I stopped at Louis's home. 'We need your help Louis, our office and John's house have just been burglarized,' I greeted him soberly.

'God, almighty!' he shouted, "What are they going to do next? Throw a bomb into our place?' When I got back to the office the first policeman had arrived. He was a polite, brawny gentleman of medium height, around forty years old. His hair was prematurely greying and three chevrons adorned his upper sleeves. During our subsequent conver-

sation it turned out that he had a master's degree in crimi-
nology. In light of this constable's personality and compe-
tence, we hoped to receive more attention and protection
from the Escondera Police.

Within the following half hour additional officers came to
our facility. Among them I believed to recognize the taller
one of those two policemen who advised John that our problems were of a civil nature, when we had last attempted to
file charges at their station. This officer entered our place
through the front door without greeting any of us, walked
straight across the office and opened the left door leading to
our shop in the back where he disappeared for a few minutes.
Afterwards he returned, using the same door again before
he turned to his colleague, who was busy with brush and
powder taking fingerprints in the right section of our facility.

'You might have lifted a couple of mine,' the constable advised his co-worker, 'I've been over there and touched some
things,' he said, indicating the left side of our office. One
of the first essentials taught in any police academy is to
advise the forensic team at the crime scene, before touching
anything, not tell them afterwards to have done so. But this
was not my main concern. The forensic work had already
been concluded in the left section of our office, before this
plain-clothes constable appeared at the scene. If any fingerprints of his were lifted, those must have been left there at
an earlier point in time.

These burglaries did not come unannounced. An employee
of Gale Cassell advised me weeks ago, that Cassell's associates were conspiring to burglarize our facility again. I re-

ported these statements to a female officer of the Escondera Police and installed an alarm system in our office. But these efforts were just as fruitless as every protective measure we had implemented against these people so far. We were obviously up against an underworld organization, committing their brazen offenses overtly and with impunity.

As if it had not already been a terrible day, Paul Stoller was suddenly loafing around our office. I could not believe my eyes. He had resigned from his directorship in our company, violated his fiduciary responsibility to my livelihood and misappropriated innumerable records of our corporation. Suddenly, here he was unannounced, hundreds of miles away from his place of residence; precisely that morning after our facility had been burglarized. I was tempted to ask him if he came down here to make sure we had been deprived of virtually all business records, but I decided to be more diplomatic. He was not about to return the documents he took from us months ago, much less did he bring our audit that we were still waiting for. Instead he invited me for a cup of coffee in a nearby restaurant.

We had barely sat down as he continued his desperate efforts to convince me of John's hand in what had happened so far. But in addition to this broken record of a speech, he suggested we should incriminate John to an extent where he could be prosecuted. I really felt like tossing the hot coffee into Paul's face, even more so after he requested a promissory note for his services pertaining to the audit we never got to see. I informed John about the contents of my last conversation with Paul after I got back.

'I hope you told this character to stuff his promissory note into a pipe and smoke it! He is acting to destroy our lives and has the nerve to demand money for doing so!'

'Why for goodness's sake is Paul behaving this way?' I just couldn't understand.

'That is a difficult subject indeed' John replied. 'We apparently ended up in the crosshairs of organized white-collar crime. These subcultures play their dreadful trade all over this country. These people often appear to be legitimate entrepreneurs engaged in perfectly legal lines of commerce, but covertly, in the background, their companies serve as money laundries, fraudulent investment schemes, distribution organizations for contraband and the like. It often takes time for our system to get wise about these types of institutions, but then eventually these organisations come under pressure and investigation from official agencies.

At that point these businesses must be dissolved rapidly and a scapegoat must be found to blame for the demise of the sham enterprise. That is exactly where we came in. That is the reason why all of our records were stolen. Those would prove our innocence and Cassell's guilt. If Paul Stoller was not part of that operation from the very start, then he is being coerced by powerful and influential people to act the way he is; He's got a lot to lose!'

'Didn't you tell me some time ago, that Cassell supposedly knows a US Senator? Could this perhaps be the insurmountable obstacle to our efforts to stop these relentless attacks?' John did not answer my question. Neither did he seem surprised about my remark. He must have arrived at the same conclusion in his attempts to find an explanation for our incredible situation.

'Do we finally have all police reports for all these burglaries?" I wanted to know.

'Not yet,' was John's reply. 'Not even a single policeman responded to my calls regarding the burglary in my house.'

'You must be kidding!' I countered.

'Unfortunately I am not. I made the honest mistake of informing the San Alberto Police, having jurisdiction over the area of my residence, that the larceny in my home was probably connected to a simultaneously committed offense in Escondera. I infer that under these circumstances San Alberto authorized the City of Escondera to handle the entire matter.'

'So we do not have any official documents regarding all three of these larcenies at all?'

'That's correct.' John returned pensively. 'Have you informed our lawyer about the current state of affairs?' I suggested. 'No, but I am doing that right now!'

It was late that afternoon when Louis showed up drunk in the office. He appeared near to a nervous breakdown. Louis had invested months of work to line up a very lucrative business venture for us, but now, after our computer had been stolen and our chances to recover the unit unscathed declining every day, the lucrative deal evaporated before our eyes so to speak, and Louis collapsed under the emotional pressure.

'I have to take Louis to a clinic; he is pacing back and forth outside, cussing and crying.' John started making his way toward the door. 'The pressure of our situation is getting too much for him. We are all in the same boat; he's just the first one to cave in. I just informed him this morning about the latest rumours spread by our adversaries. I'm supposed to be a drug dealer and notorious swindler with Cassell being my latest victim. You're a mentally retarded illegal alien, and Louis's some type of crook and pervert. That's what I've heard coming down the grapevine. Fred had the kindness to submit his resignation in light of the circumstances. And by the way, Dan Health just threatened over the phone to send some Negroes my way, to rape my thirteen year old daughter, who used to call him Uncle Dan.'

I did not even want to reply to this and remained silent. In the subsequent days John brought his family to his parents in law, somewhere north of Los Angeles. Unfortunately they were not safe up there either. John's teenage daughter was walking home from school when a large sedan suddenly drove up onto the sidewalk, blocking her way. She had been forewarned by her family, reacted immediately and jumped a garden fence screaming for help. Witnesses stated that a black man was driving that car. The incident was brought to the attention of the local police, right along with the according threats issued, but nothing happened, as usual.

Our corporate legal counsel appeared totally flabbergasted over our situation, yet unable to react to incidents of this magnitude and frequency. John's desperate pleas to an ever-increasing number of government agencies were in vain, and my efforts to obtain help and protection from my consulate were just as fruitless.

A few days thereafter John arrived at the office with more bad news. 'Rumours are making the rounds that you murdered your own mother,' he told me with a staggered expression on his face. 'Aside from that, death threats have just been issued against the both of us!' I didn't even want to know the source of this information. Its origin was obvious. 'We are still experiencing problems with the mail; our postal shipments are coming in late or not at all.'

'Could it be that the Escondera Police is interfering with our mail?'

'No way,' John countered. 'Only the federal government may by court order tamper with postal shipments!' Unfortunately years later, a federal agent advised me that the local police may access the mail service. – A possible retrospective explanation for the problem at issue.

After a year had passed since my application, my Treaty – Investor E – Visa was finally approved. But instead of a visa – seal imprint in my passport I received merely a slip of paper confirming my lawful presence in the USA for one year. To my amazement I realized that I still could not just leave and re-enter the USA. This was one more aspect of the international friendship convention to wonder about.

Our Business had shrunk to a mere few trucks on the road. Our troubles made their rounds in the business community. We kept working for second rate customers who paid their bills late or not at all. John and I worked for hardly more than expense money to keep us afloat. 'Have you finally received burglary reports from the Escondera Police?' I asked John almost on a weekly basis. 'No, I am getting the run-around from this department, but I got an appointment at the state attorney's office next week to file a complaint against the city of Escondera.' He was packing his briefcase. 'It's Saturday noon, I'll be back Monday, I just need to spend some time with my loved ones,' John advised me as he got up from his chair. 'Right on,' I said. 'Have a nice weekend. I'll hang around for a couple more hours.'

Soon thereafter the phone rang. It was Louis.

'I need help,' he was stammering as he told me that he had just been removed from hospital-care by Escondera Police personnel and was then interrogated at their headquarters. 'They threatened to lock me up if I wouldn't incriminate you and John,' he continued, 'and Don Bricklin is at the police station disassembling what appears to be left of our missing computer system!'

I closed the office and rushed to John's house, in hopes that he had already arrived. He just had and, instead of taking out his family for lunch, he went straight to the clinic to visit Louis. The following Monday he took off to the Escondera Police Department. When he came back he looked pale and was shaking. He continued to the bathroom where he had to throw up. I just kept looking at him without saying a word. 'My dear God, I just cannot believe all this here is really happening, I have never seen our system act this way!' He was now clearly in despair.

'I have just been told that we are not getting police reports respective to the burglaries or any offenses in which we were the victims. The Escondera Police will henceforth take the position of having no knowledge of any wrongdoing committed against you, me or our corporation. Should we submit any insurance claims, the City of Escondera will implement measures to have us charged with insurance fraud. That is what I just got told at the police station.' He was frantically rubbing his forehead at this stage. 'We must leave this city, and file a suit against it,' John decided. 'You must contact your embassy for protection. I must try to get help from the FBI.'

I felt like I was watching a twisted, devious plot unfold. Everything around me seemed surreal, almost like a story from one of those Hitchcock films, where average, law-abiding people suddenly and unsuspectingly find themselves surrounded by a strange, frightening world where they do not belong.

I'd found it, – the dark side of America. The same gloomy feeling came over me as it had done for inexplicable reasons during my very first evening in this nation. But this time it was not about to disappear the subsequent morning. It was meant to stay for a long, long time.

CHAPTER FOUR

In the meantime, an Escondera Police Officer, accompanied by Don Bricklin paid a visit to Louis' parents. The elderly couple appeared to have been unambiguously advised by their visitors about the allegedly unsavoury characters of John Sullivan and myself. As a result, the friendly American retirees withdrew their commitments for funds to establish our insurance business in partnership with Louis Martin. Louis moved to northern California where he started a new life.

One afternoon I was alone in the office, when I saw Don Bricklin's automobile pulling into the parking lot. Our former computer specialist was obviously about to make a purchase in the neighbouring auto parts store. I stepped outside and stood in front of his car. 'Don,' I started, 'were you involved in burglaries committed against our business?' Bricklin seemed stunned, and answered almost obediently. 'Yes, Gale Cassell offered me several thousand dollars to deprive your business of whatever might incriminate him.'

'You could have gotten caught,' I returned. A smirk came over Don's face.

'Let's say I got caught long before I broke into your place!' then Don continued to insinuate having committed this burglary right under the eyes of the police. 'Don, do you mean to tell me that police were here at the scene when you burglarized our office?' Bricklin's facial expression became very serious as he bowed his head forward and seemed to be looking insistently at the pavement in front of his shoes. As he finally lifted his head, his eyes were wide open. A loud and clear 'Yes!' was accompanied by his expressive nodding. Whether Don had ever told a lie in his life, I do not know, but what I had just heard from him was undoubtedly the truth. Then Bricklin's self assertiveness began to return. 'Sullivan ought to be careful; otherwise he might end up in jail.' He concluded our conversation and went about his business.

There was no police seal posted at our door the morning after the burglary. We had to call the police rather than vice-versa. So this alleged presence of police at our office the night of the burglary had to be of a truly unofficial nature. And the remarkable behaviour of the constable, who obviously left his fingerprints in our facility before the police arrived at the scene, was explicable. But it was still difficult for me to believe that law enforcement officers in a town in southern California would dare to engage in misconduct of this magnitude, without the approval from high-ranking government agencies, or exceptionally influential and very powerful individuals.

Meanwhile we had to file for creditor's protection ourselves. John dispatched our few remaining vehicles from a little office in his house. We closed our facility in Escondera permanently. John continued relentlessly to ask government agencies for help, but was continually met with stoic indifference. His patriotic feelings were gradually confronted with very unpleasant aspects of his home country, for which he fought in Vietnam. – America; love it or hate it, just never underestimate it!

John and I filed lawsuits against the City of Escondera at the regional California superior court building. John contacted several lawyers, specialized in civil rights issues. Among them was a regionally renowned attorney with considerable experience in precisely this field of law. According to John, this gentleman was not merely interested, but right out enthused about our case and seemed to be rubbing his hands eager to bring this matter before the courts.

John had obviously not informed this attorney that I was a foreign national. It was apparently after this lawyer realized that I did not have US citizenship, when his interest in our case declined substantially. At that time I attributed this circumstance to the mere difficulty of winning a judgment on behalf of an alien against an established, American community. However, the issue seemed to be more complex, as I would soon find out.

I kept looking through the windshield, my hands holding the broad steering wheel. The big diesel engine was growling beside me as the sixty foot semi-truck rolled along on the freeway. The change of scenery should have cleared my head, but the idyllic landscape whizzing by my windows brought me at best a superficial peace of mind. Our monumental problems accompanied me on my routes to Boston, Seattle and Miami like a bad co-driver. And my pleasant encounters with innumerable polite and friendly Americans were of little help to improve my overall situation. Yet I had done no wrong to anybody in the USA, neither had our corporation. I'd never had a criminal record in my life. I'd left my last job in Europe, in an armoured transportation business, on my own terms with an excellent reference.

I was always oriented pro-American; I'd invested foreign funds into this nation and created employment and income for its people. There was no objective reason for animosity against my presence here. My home country enjoyed an excellent relationship with the USA, but there had to be some peculiar element of political or judicial origin, turning my American dream into a nightmare.

John accompanied me to see my consul in Los Angeles. I was received by a distinguished, polite diplomat of my country. The well-dressed gentleman seemed surprised, if not to say perturbed, over my statements. He repeatedly shook his head, but when I was done he kept looking at the surface of his desk and remained silent for almost a minute. After raising his head again, he replied with a fatherly undertone in his voice. 'Here we happen to be standing on foreign soil, and…' he expressed a degree of helplessness in his voice and expression, 'you know, these treaties with the USA…, those have merely historical value these days.'

I suppose my reply should have been why for God's sake were international conventions of merely historical significance still in force, instead of being displayed in the showcase of a museum, where they belong. But I suppose, the answer would have been just as diplomatically evasive as the statement I'd just received. Was my country afraid to forfeit bilateral agreements with a superpower? Were other aspects of great importance connected to this treaty, which needed to be renegotiated upon cancelling that convention? I had great difficulty believing that my native homeland would send its citizens deliberately into the trap of a foreign nation.

The diplomatic interpretation regarding the status of this international agreement raised my curiosity. I felt as if I had found a trace leading to the key to unravelling the puzzle of my bizarre situation in the USA. I consulted another experienced civil rights attorney in the region, and briefed him about my experiences in this country. This time I pointed unambiguously at my rights, including the last paragraph of the Amendment XIV;

No state shall… deny to any person under its jurisdiction the equal protection of the laws.

Inadvertently, I seemed to have touched upon a controversial subject. The lawyers eyes drifted over to the left side of his desk and his head also turned in that direction. He started to fumble around with some objects nearby his telephone. His efforts to avoid eye contact with me were very obvious as he replied somewhat embarrassed, 'That applies only to US citizens.'

Well, that was news to me. When did this law come into effect and how could it be that the world is apparently unaware of this deplorable state of affairs? Why are treaties entered with innumerable countries around the globe stating otherwise? Were cosignatory nations informed about this change of statutes? If so, why don't they advise their citizens that civil rights and investments by foreigners are unprotected by US law? And where were the United Nations and the media? I could not even divulge these findings to my friends. That the United States of America had clandestinely curtailed essential human rights for foreigners seemed so incredible; nobody would believe me. I had to keep this to myself, until it was verified beyond a doubt. And that was not exactly going to be easy.

I was on my way back from the east coast, I had not slept for a couple of days and I hadn't had time to sit down for a good hearty meal. So when I reached the lovely little town of Lordsburg, tucked away in the Table Mountains of New Mexico, the inevitable desire for a hot meal and a comfortable bed in a cool motel room came over me. It was summertime and the temperature in the region rarely dropped below twenty-five degrees Celsius at night. The motel by the name of 'Spanish Trail' was small, and its adjacent restaurant was tiny, but the two friendly ladies operating the place treated me very hospitably. The subsequent morning I was well rested to continue my journey. 'We'll see you on your next trip,' one of the two motel managers called over to me, as I started the engine and slowly turned on to the highway.

However, there was no next trip. It was to become my last. John told me that he went obediently, as recommended by the law, to the city assembly of Escondera, where he orderly announced his suit against that community. He was arrested right at the podium and spent several days in jail. In the meantime our remaining contractors took off to look for work elsewhere. As a consequence, our company finally collapsed and we had to give up our last vehicle. I still see the truck before my eyes, slowly pulling away from me, with John at the steering wheel, nearby his house in the northern suburb of San Alberto.

Unfortunately that house was not about to be his much

longer. He took out a loan on his property to keep us afloat, but was unable to pay the interest due on the mortgage and, after the loss of their home, his wife took up drinking. 'The Escondera Police grimly asked me about your current place of residence,' John advised me a couple of days later. 'I told them, that I had no idea where you were.'

My creditor overseas was in no way pleased about our situation, but he was a good, old family friend. He lent me an additional amount of money to buy a taxicab in order to survive until this entire matter could be resolved. However my proposed career as a taxi driver in San Alberto ended before it began. My driver's license had been officially cancelled. The reason seemed to be a couple of traffic infraction tickets, which remained unpaid, after we had to leave Escondera almost overnight. John arranged the payments for the tickets, but my license was revoked permanently it seemed and John's efforts to have it reinstated were in vain.

I never drove under the influence of alcohol. I never endangered anybody on an American roadway. As a matter of fact, I was never involved in an accident in the USA. All the same, my driving permit was gone for good. The suits John and I filed a while ago were rejected, primarily over hair splitting judicial pretences; in my case mostly for my omission to appear before the city assembly, which I was obviously frightened to comply with in light of John's arrest.

It seemed advisable for me to move from my current place of residence, where I'd lived since the foundation of our business. So I rented a space for an old travel trailer I bought a couple of years ago, in a valley leading up to the coastal range. I had to trade in my newly acquired taxi for an old station wagon and a little bit of cash to survive for a while.

Alpina was a little town of maybe a couple of thousand inhabitants. The charming village was nestled in a plateau embedded on the left side of the valley. A tiny but steep mountain rose amidst the scenery, surrounded by a small American Native Reservation with a cattle ranch. As in most parts of southern California, relatively few trees adorned the landscape. The rest of the vegetation consisted mostly of grass bushels and shrubs. The grounds were made up of sandy earth and reddish, beige coloured rocks. The regional population lived predominately in family homes, tucked away in the surrounding areas of the hillsides. It was a nice and quiet region. Only at night the coyotes held their howling spectacle. Sometimes they entered the R.V. Park looking for food, tossing over the trashcans. During the day golden eagles were gracefully turning their circles over the mountain lands, and California's sunshine provided pleasant temperatures on a daily basis.

It was in fall when John informed me that Don Bricklin had passed away. According to John's information, Don had suffered a heart attack or stroke somewhere in central California. Sudden death may strike anybody, including a man in his forties in good overall health, like Bricklin. But since he was allegedly accompanied by Dan Health when it happened, his death of natural causes appeared somewhat doubtful. Don might have been only a minor actor in an extensive series of criminal offenses, but when those involved have an official capacity and dabble in organized crime, – then it can be deadly.

Around that time I received a letter from my consul. It appeared that my consulate did contact the City of Escondera after all. And the consul got the following response:

We are in receipt of your letter, requesting information about one of your citizens (Harry Burger). A review of our files indicates that this office has not had contact with (Mr. Burger). It appears that a business associate of (Mr. Burger), one (John Sullivan) attempted to file a lawsuit against the city of (Escondera). That suit was filed in the superior court of the north county district in (San Alberto) under case number N 20 721.

Prior to the filing of the lawsuit, Mr. (Sullivan) attempted to file a claim with the City of (Escondera) for the damages to his reputation which occurred during a police investigation of an alleged burglary of his residence and business. We infer that Mr. (Burger's) relationship to this matter is that he was a business associate of Mr. (Sullivan) and apparently owned some part of the business which was allegedly burglarized. The claim against the City of (Escondera) was founded upon what Mr. (Sullivan) regarded to be unjust allegations relating to the burglary.

The particulars thereof are confidential under California state law and cannot be released without the concurrence of all the parties involved. However, the claim filed alleges that in August and September of 1981, that one Detective (B.) allowed a confessed burglar to set up a computer owned by Mr. (Sullivan) and conduct a search of its mem-

ory. Mr. (Sullivan) alleges that this improper use of the computer and a subsequent refusal to release it to him deprived his company of the use of the computer from September, (through February the subsequent year).

Shortly afterward it was determined that the claim which had been filed on behalf of Mr. (Sullivan) was tardy. Petitions to file a late claim were subsequently denied. Thereafter, the lawsuit referred to above ensued. At this point it does not appear that Mr. (Burger) ever joined in any lawsuit nor independently ever filed any claim or suit against the City of (Escondera). It also appears at this time that the suit filed by Mr. (Sullivan) was defective and was never pursued by that individual. For those reasons, the City of (Escondera) regards this matter as being a closed case.

Signed: M. S. (Escondera) Police Department.

Since I stood right in front of John when the two of us filed those lawsuits, and I was first at the wicket in the court building, my suit bares the number N 20 720. I subsequently obtained a copy of that lawsuit from the court, and the imprint of a rubber seal with the words "SUMMONS ISSUED", which left no doubts that this suit had been filed and served. For those reasons it was virtually impossible that the city at issue would have been unaware of it. A public official misleading a foreign consul in his attempts to protect one of his citizens abroad is a remarkable act, if not to say outrageous. I sent a copy of that suit to my consul, in vague hopes that this undeniable proof might awaken the diplomats of my country from their sleepy way of life.

After five years in coastal southern California my chronic breathing problems had completely disappeared. These appreciable improvements in my health would have, under normal circumstances, been plenty of reason for a real celebration. However, the situation I found myself in had totally diminished any inkling of festive mood. Asides from my legal and economic situation, I seemed to have exchanged my allergies for high blood pressure, chronic headaches, nightmares that robbed me of my sleep and a tinnitus that sounded as if an old freight train was driving around my head with its brakes applied.

John fortunately recovered from a half sided nervous facial palsy, and he had to leave the state for a while to temporarily disassociate himself from our situation. This three-year battle against the "good" and bad guys collectively took a heavy toll on our health and there was still no proverbial light at the other end of the tunnel. I felt just as guilty over John's plight as he did over mine. If the two of us had never met in the first place it would have been to the advantage of us both. But this is beside the point. We were just unsuspectingly in the wrong place at the wrong time.

In the meantime I began to address the government for help on my own and eventually managed to get an F.B.I. agent on the telephone. This gentleman concluded that it was unfair. – By no means was it unfair the way this country had treated me so far, but rather it was unfair of me to make such allegations! Apparently, I had the opportunity to become accustomed to all kinds of niceties from the civilian as well as the official side in this nation. This reply felt like a kick in the stomach and left me wondering what I had done to deserve such a retort, perhaps my foreign accent?

It was down to selling my travel trailer, or starvation. Of course I decided for the former option. It did not take long to find a buyer and I was watching my temporary home pulling onto the highway, coupled to the pickup truck of its new owner. With my few remaining earthly belongings stashed in my old station wagon I cruised down the valley, only a couple of hours later. Alpina began to retreat in my rear view mirror. I was bound for San Martino, the southern suburb of San Alberto where I had resided most of the time since my arrival in this country. Some miles down the road I bought a hamburger and a couple of donuts. Then I continued until I reached the seashore.

The evening sun had laid its glistening veil over the Pacific Ocean and little waves darted smoothly upon its calm, flat shore. A few seagulls were sailing in the mild evening breeze, and somewhere in the distance I heard music coming from a radio. Yet most beachgoers had already left the area. I was sitting behind the wheel of my parked car, almost unaware of the world around me. I just kept gazing at the empty horizon in front of me, until its contours disappeared in the darkness of the night.

CHAPTER FIVE

The system of the United States of America is characterized by utter complexity: Federal, State, County and City jurisdictions exist parallel to each other, particularly in aspects of law enforcement. The government mechanism of this country was once meticulously conceived, and continually amended. Based upon its size of territory and population the jurisdiction of individual government agencies are cautiously divided and assigned to improve overall control and efficiency. But in very large countries like the USA, a once properly functioning government apparatus has contorted into a huge, puzzling maze with little transparency for the public and vast opportunities for the state to send average people into an eternal run-around. Every system of a commonwealth is only as good as the people operating it.

US American jurisprudence is not predominately marked by this pragmatic and almost sober approach to right and wrong, as customary within most of Western Europe today. US courts of law reflect a somewhat more traditional approach to justice, with a tendency towards feudal grandeur, solemnity and authority; if not to say displays of omnipotence. Emotional aspects seemed often just as important as the principles of right and wrong. The shrewdness of a top-notch lawyer and the flamboyancy of his summing up are of greater significance than in the old world. The fees for professional legal counsel are usually higher, partly due to the complexity of US Law, sometimes almost bordering on contradiction.

Lawyers in the USA tend to specialize in particular fields of law, chiefly criminal defence, civil rights, corporate law, immigration, business litigation and so forth. A considerable part of their work seems to consist of research; for the most part finding precedent court rulings, for cases similar to those of their clients. Innumerable law students earn pocket money by doing such research in America's huge law libraries. Rights for the American public are principally provided by the law, but if civil rights have been violated by official capacity, the burden of proof rests upon the victim. Civil rights violations perpetrated by public officials appear to be committed on a much larger scale in the USA than in most European nations, and often with a much higher degree of severity. Since the government is manifestly liable for such abuse of state power, it has little incentive to investigate these incidents properly.

Legal aid institutions exist all over this country. These provide jurisprudential support for the less fortunate segments of the population and are mostly funded by private donations. Yet these institutions are usually hopelessly overloaded with cases and the chances for getting any help from these establishments are slim.

The principles of law enforcement are very essential to any society. Policemen personify authority and they are entitled to use force if necessary. Superior government agencies are in charge to overview police and to intervene in cases where police powers are abused. This principle often exists just in theory and in numerous parts of the USA law enforcement has developed an eerie dynamic of its own. It appears that mostly city policemen are the culprits in severe cases of misconduct, followed by county deputy sheriffs; federal agents seem to be third in line, and law enforcement officers under the direct jurisdiction of one of the individual states have, as it seems, the lowest incident rate of malfeasance.

States with very large metropolitan areas, as well as those known for religious conservatism seem to be most vulnerable to being affected by severe misconduct of their servants. The large amounts of money circulating in big cities seem to draw organized crime, unsavoury politicians and dishonest public officials from all over the country. Religious fundamentalists sometimes tend to put personal convictions above the law. This mentality may also affect regional government agencies and lead to commission of improprieties.

Organized crime has its own peculiarities within this nation. In most European countries those subcultures lead a rather shadowy life, marked by outward restraint and discretion. Their US counterparts appear to make amazingly little efforts to hide. Innumerable legitimate enterprises of various natures all over the United States allegedly belong to the underworld. Those are usually funded by investments earned by illicit means.

The acceptance of the US Mafia by the broad population in the USA might be based upon their bootlegging activities during the nineteen twenties. During the prohibition in those years the underworld provided the supply of illegal liquor to the public. Around the same era, organized crime provided their muscle to trade unions for their fight against inadequate labour laws. In doing so the underworld earned their appreciation from large segments of the American public.

Yet the US system may have its own motives for a peaceful coexistence with these subcultures. It seems at best an open secret that US intelligence agencies joined forces with the underworld in the nineteen sixties to eliminate a Latin American head of state. Although this endeavour remained unsuccessful, it appeared to provide organized crime with a quasi right to exist, if not to say legitimacy.

It must be anticipated that this was not the first, much less the last, time the system of the USA resorted to these dark forces in order to solve problems that could not be handled by legislature and judiciary. As a consequence, considerable segments of criminal activities within the United States of America are no longer merely organized but essentially institutionalized. All these factors are particularly problematic for unsuspecting foreigners coming from highly developed European countries, convinced that they are well covered by the laws of a democratic state of rights. On the other hand foreign government representatives must, in their efforts to protect their citizens within the USA, tread very carefully upon the territory of this superpower. Diplomats are not inclined to man the barricades for ordinary people, much less within a huge, powerful country. Harmonious political relationships with large, important nations are unfortunately of much greater importance than the rights of an ordinary citizen abroad. In the face of these circumstances I decided to attempt complaining to the US foreign ministry, the US Department of State on my very own, and I got a letter back:

Dear (Sir)

This responds to your letter of November 7, concerning reverses sustained in your business affairs in California. I note that you have brought this matter to the attention of (your) Consul in Los Angeles.

This office has no law enforcement authority. The courts of the United States and those of California have demonstrated over many years a readiness to protect the legal rights of aliens, as well as citizens, in the United States, including treaty rights, if applicable. According you may wish to retain competent private legal counsel and pursue whatever remedies may be available in the courts.

Signed: H. C. U.S. Department of State

Since the statutes of the "U.N. Charta of Human Rights" specify protection under the laws, I wrote to the United Nations Organization. Their reply was brief and clear:

Dear (Sir)

This is to acknowledge the receipt of your communication which has been read with attention. I regret to inform you that the Secretariat of the United Nations is not in a position to be of assistance to you in the matter raised in your communication.

J. M. U. N. Centre for Human Rights, Geneva

Nevertheless, these accumulating replies were better than nothing, which was exactly what I got back as a reaction to about nine out of every ten written requests for help and protection. Meanwhile I also had to become accustomed to having the phone hung up at my Embassy and Consulate and their unwillingness to answer my letters. Even the media showed no interest in our case and additional lawyers I contacted were shrugging their shoulders and reacted evasively to my question regarding the applicability of the Constitutional Amendment XIV to foreigners. John had already been knocking on the doors of dozens of government offices without avail; now it was my turn to experience this deliberate indifference of the US System, after it had already turned both of our lives upside down. The two of us had decided to terminate mutual contact, particularly on account of violent threats issued against the both of us. Aside from that, John had virtually done everything he could to help me.

The answer I received to my letter that I wrote to the U.S. Attorney General amounted to nothing, but it was nonetheless somewhat more emphatic:

Dear (Sir)

Your letter and enclosures to the Attorney General concerning allegations of breach of contract, fraud, embezzlement, and other unlawful acts committed against your company (...) by (...) and various other individuals have been referred to me. You also allege malfeasance on the part of the (Escondera) Police Department.

As you may know, Federal Intervention is warranted only where there is evidence that there has been a violation of Federal laws. Unfortunately, your letter and enclosures do not provide sufficient evidence of any Federal violation to support intervention. Furthermore, the matters about which you are concerned involve state, rather than Federal jurisdiction.

The Federal Bureau of Investigation (FBI) is the investigative agency of this department. I can only suggest that if you have evidence of a violation of Federal law that you present it to the local office of the FBI for evaluation. I must stress, however, that the FBI may only act where there is proper federal jurisdiction, which does not appear to exist from any of the material you have submitted to this department.

I am sorry, but there does not appear to be any way in which we may appropriately be of assistance to you at this time.

Sincerely G. N. Attorney, US Department of Justice

Since "these matters involve state, rather than federal jurisdiction" I wrote to the California State Attorney's offices. I enclosed the usual documents, including statements from John Sullivan and Louis Martin with the following text:

I, (John Sullivan) confirm herewith that I was the Chairman of the board of Directors (of a Corporation owned by Mr. Harry Burger). As such I witnessed the Investment by

Mr. (Burger) and (his fellow Countryman Associate) of over $ 300,000 in said business. Mr. (Burger) made such investment on the advice of, and within the guidelines described by his attorney, M. F. W. with the intentions of establishing a "bona fide" enterprise which created employment for U.S. citizens. Mr. (Burger's) uppermost concern in the building of this new business was to conform with any and all of our laws concerning the conduct of foreign investors under the treaty investor program.

I further witnessed an orchestrated attack on (that business), Mr. (Burger) and myself, which attack was perpetrated by former associates of this venture, and which included embezzlement, fraud, theft, libel, slander and ultimately burglary. And which attack was materially aided by the actions of at least one official agency, the (Escondera) Police Department. This agency refused the corporation, Mr. (Burger) and myself, the protections guaranteed by our constitution. Moreover this agency actually assisted the attackers in their libellous activities, and publicly endorsed the commission of a burglary against (said Business). I truly believe that a criminal conspiracy existed by and between our former associates and members of the (Escondera) Police Department, including at least one Detective (B.)

The net result of these crimes, and prejudicial actions by a public agency, was to deny (our Business) access to and use of the tools and relationships needed to continue in business. The company's computer was stolen, records stolen, and the reputation in the community destroyed with the assistance of the aforementioned public agency.

The records, cash and equipment stolen has not as of this day turned up. However, the computer did turn up in the possession of the (Escondera) Police Department and our efforts to claim our property were thwarted by this agency.

These facts are just a small piece of the information which I feel points to a conspiracy against the interests of (mentioned Corporation) and its principals Mr. (Burger) and myself. I feel the constitutional rights of the corporation, and Mr. (Burger) were seriously violated by these conditions.

In summary a (European) citizen, making every effort to conform with U.S. Law was swindled, slandered, burglarized and held up to public ridicule with the assistance of a public agency. His constitutional rights were violated and in the end he was left in poverty and with a legal nightmare of monumental proportions.

Signed: "John Sullivan"-.

Louis Martin also made the following statement of accounts:

The following is my statement of those facts and circumstances which I am personally aware of regarding the affairs of (the business of Mr. Burger) and its officers and staff. My relationship was one of economic consultant to (said business) and its principal investors Mr. (Harry Burger) and (John Sullivan).

I first became associated with (that business) in December of 1980 at which time I was hired for the purpose of building a corporate insurance agency to specialize in casualty lines relating to the transportation business. I was to supply the required license and insurance expertise and (Mr. Burger's Company) the required funds to launch a subsidiary venture with myself as its president. Unfortunately as a direct result of (Mr. Burger's) Company's deteriorating condition our agency was never completed.

During the period of my association with (said business) the company and both, Mr. (Sullivan) and Mr. (Burger) treated me exceptionally well, and I further observed that they treated all personnel in a similar manner. In fact they offered financial subsidies to most of their key personnel including those mentioned herein.

I was personally present for (that company's) directors' meeting involving the full board of directors, with the exception of Mr. (Paul Stoller) who resided elsewhere and was not present for the meetings I attended. In the course of said meetings the plans and day-to-day operations were discussed.

(Mr. Burger's) Company entered into a joint operating agreement with one (Gale Cassell), debtor in possession of (a corporation), which called for certain joint venture operations. (Soon) it became apparent that this "joint venture" was ill advised as the (personnel of that business) was unable to meet any of their commitments to (Mr. Burger's) company, and their chief operating officer (Gale Cassell) was acting to create division within (Mr. Burger's) Com-

pany's staff and directors. It was ultimately decided to ter-minate this operation.

With the dissolution of the joint venture, a disagreement with several of the officers occurred. Most notably Mr. (Dan Health) who it appeared had been engaged in con-flicts of interest in that he intentionally violated corporate policy and directives to the benefit of Mr. (Cassell) and (his enterprise). Subsequent to the dissolution, I witnessed an attack against (Mr. Burger's Company) and its investors, which consisted of unfounded allegations, innuendo, and libel, directed to (Mr. Burger's Corporation's) creditors and valued business contacts.

As a result of this circumstance, I found myself in a posi-tion of having elected to sever past associations in favour of a future, which never materialized. The stress involved was too much for me and I went off the wagon and ul-timately required hospitalization in an alcoholic recov-ery program. During this time period the facilities of Mr. (Burger's) Business were broken into and property, records, and cash were taken, which included the computer (Mr. Burger's Business) had purchased from one (Don Bricklin) / Matchmaker Technology.

In September (that year) I was admitted to the De-Tox pro-gram at (a) Hospital. The expense of this hospitalization treatment was provided by (Mr. Burger's Company) and its chairman, (John Sullivan) who was personally respon-sible for convincing me to take this course of action. On September the second I was contacted at that hospital by a detective (B.) and Sergeant from the (Escondera) Police De-

partment who made it apparent that I had little choice but to accompany them to the police station for questioning. I was surprised to find that at the police station one (Don Bricklin), who was the prime suspect in the aforementioned burglary, was not only present and operating the missing computer (of Mr. Burger's Company) but was actually allowed to participate in my questioning.

The questioning revolved around allegations that Mr. (Sullivan) was a dope dealer, and was allegedly involved with Mr. (Cassell) in a tax shelter fraud and that Mr. (Burger) was retarded or at least not competent. I was offered immunity if I would help incriminate Mr. (Sullivan). I declined, explaining that (Mr. Burger and his company and Mr. Sullivan) had been exceptionally kind to me personally.

During the period immediately prior to my admission to (the hospital) I was working on a program to contract with Mexican based carriers to perform the stateside legs of their international shipments. This venture required an exceptionally high paper load which could not be effectively handled without the computer, and which would require additional investments by (Mr. Burger's Company). As a direct result of the crimes committed against (Mr. Burger's Corporation) they were rendered unable to go forward on this program, and suffered an additional loss of revenues, and a direct loss of my fees and expenses in setting the transaction up which approximated $ 10,000. Not to mention the time and efforts invested by other staff personnel. It appeared that the loss of this transaction was the proverbial straw that broke the camels back for (Mr. Burger's Business). In summary I witnessed a series of crimes *against (Mr. Burger's Company), Mr. (Burger), and Mr. (Sullivan), which rendered them bankrupt and which apparently had the full cooperation of the (Escondera) Police Department. In fact I am aware that the personal attacks, which included violent threats, continued well into 1982.*

This statement is made of my own free will, and I certify the contents to be true and correct to the best of my knowledge and belief;

Signed: "Louis Martin"-.

In the subsequent weeks I got a phone call from a Deputy California State Attorney General. Unfortunately the gentlemen advised me that his superior would not let him investigate this matter, although he personally would like to do so. The text of his follow up letter was very brief;

Dear (Sir)

Pursuant to our conversation, I am returning your materials.

Very truly yours, S. F. Deputy Attorney General, Department of Justice, State of California

I had, of course also submitted correspondence with enclosures to the District Attorney's office in San Alberto, after John Sullivan unsuccessfully tried to get help from this government agency; unfortunately without any success. As time passed, I became aware that legal cases indicating government misconduct and possible involvement of organized crime were met with notorious rejection by the US system. What never must happen simply does not happen; so let's pretend it never really happened in the first place.

Rumours have it that very high ranking politicians could be on the payroll of the US Underworld and nobody, may he be a government employee, a lawyer or a news reporter wanted to end up in the crosshairs of organized crime or corrupt police, much less take a risk in being put out of favour by people in the highest levels of the federal government. As a consequence I found myself with my back against the wall.

My visa had expired and in light of my situation it did not seem advisable attempting to have it renewed. Under normal circumstances the renewal of my visa would have been a mere formality, but my circumstances were anything but normal. I had lost my investments in two livelihoods and my driver's license on top of it. But worst of all, I did not have any bona fide evidence to substantiate wrongdoing committed against me and our corporation, since an entire series of criminal offenses had been covered up – one by one – with official capacity. Therewith I was facing possible criminal charges upon return to my home country for misappropriation of funds, embezzlement or fraud, based upon the loss of those loans from overseas.

My first visits to the New World left me with the impression of friendly, courteous and peaceful inhabitants of the USA, striving for justice, equality, freedom and mutual respect. This superpower had just lost the Vietnam War, the national self-esteem had suffered, and America was licking its wounds. I anticipated the liberal era of the seventies to be a forward oriented course that this country was aiming for. Unfortunately this mind-set was about to end with this very decade, and a tidal wave of patriotism, accompanied by religious fundamentalism, suddenly swept across the nation.

As a side effect, the values and standing of anything foreign declined substantially. Immigrants were being met increasingly with reluctance, if not to say aversion; including those from Europe. And foreigners became increasingly subjects of discrimination. America had always been a God fearing land, but the form of religiosity spreading across the nation around the eighties appeared distinct from traditional values. It seemed almost superficial in nature and rather based upon pretence than true devotion and sincerity. However, those were not the only changes the US society underwent in those days.

Unsavoury opportunism used to be ostracized by the broad public, until it became fashionable at that time. Ruthless profiteers were suddenly heralded as modern day heroes. Fairness, honesty and respect for others were increasingly regarded as quaint. Decent entrepreneurs were almost scoffed at for being old fashioned. A decline in quality of consumer products became evident as a consequence. Organized crime appeared to be in its heydays, and schemes of an ever increasing number of white collar crooks began to overburden the justice system. It almost seemed as if the entire USA were speeding down the fast lane. Turbulent times lay ahead for America, as well as for me.

San Martino received me with bright sunshine on a typical mid summer day. I rented a humble room in a cheap motel not far away from my former place of residence. I could not really explain my motives for returning to this border town. In the few years I had resided here, the village served me as a mere place to rest. I spent my daily life at the business, miles away, and I had no emotional ties to the place. Yet I almost felt at home amidst the familiar surroundings. On the other hand it might have been my bad experience with Anglo American culture.

San Martino was mostly populated by Latin Americans and I felt more comfortable among people who did not remind me of those responsible for my situation. Yet it was a poor folks place and was regarded as a high crime ghetto by the established society of San Alberto. For me it was a rough landing upon rugged terrain, but I arrived at the right place nonetheless. Mexican-Americans did not seem to mind if somebody was from Alabama or from Albania and many of them, like me, did not have a valid permit to live here.

As I was sauntering down the San Martino Boulevard I realized that I had never really walked around here in all these years. My friends advised me repeatedly that this area was somewhat dangerous. But smugglers, pickpockets and drug dealers were the least of my worries in those days. If you aint got nothing left, you aint got much to loose. So I kept walking down the streets as if they were the safest place on earth. One to three story buildings lined the main road on both sides, some with little shops on the ground floor and residential space above. San Martino's Mexican flair had its own charm, although the area looked admittedly modest.

Actually it was a southern enclave of the City of San Alberto with only a few thousand inhabitants. Yet it offered about twelve motels, three large supermarkets, halve a dozen fast food eateries, several family restaurants and two drugstores. San Martino was one of the busiest border crossings in the world. Its shopping facilities catered predominately to inhabitants from the large Mexican City, right across the border. Most suburbs in the western United States stretched over miles, and were made up of nothing but one family homes. San Martino offered practically everything within walking distance and it was possible to get around without an automobile. This was an advantage for me, since I needed to limit my driving to bare necessity. The continuously rising prices for gasoline were one reason, my revoked driving license being the other.

After I turned around on my little stroll at the international border, which I was no longer able to cross, I sat down on a little bench for a while and enjoyed the scenery before walking back to the motel. From a distance the houses appeared to be shaking in the Californian summer heat. A fine layer of brownish dust covered the leaves of the eucalyptus trees along the streets. The air was dry, but pleasantly enriched with a tiny trace of salt from the Pacific Ocean; its shores only a few miles away.

'Hello stranger! Where have you been?' Linda, the pretty cashier in the supermarket greeted me, as I stood before her with a few groceries in my basket. 'I just needed a change of scenery for a while, but I am glad to be back home,' I replied with a friendly smile. I had just reached the age of thirty seven that day and finally achieved fluency as well as a moderate articulacy in English after six continuous years in California. But Spanish was the unofficial Language of San Martino; English was seldom heard around this town. So I went to look for some books to learn Spanish. I'd already had to learn one foreign language over here; I might as well learn a second while I'm at it.

The wounds of a terrible massacre in San Martino had still not entirely healed. It was only a couple of days after I moved to Alpina a year ago, when an unemployed Anglo American security guard seemed to have lost his mind. He allegedly uttered the words "I am going to hunt humans," before the heavily armed middle aged man opened fire at everybody in sight within a fast food restaurant. When he was eventually shot dead by police officers, over a dozen people, women and children among them, lay lifeless in their blood. The fast food chain had since moved their branch to a new location. The old building got torn down and a small schoolhouse was built in its place. A number of small marble pillars, surrounded by a tiny, symbolical iron fence, were erected at the scene to commemorate the sad event.

The media reported that the perpetrator most likely acted out of discontent over his unemployment, but I had my doubts about this explanation. The murderer lived with his wife and children in short walking distance from the crime scene in a nice apartment and called two automobiles his own. Looking around the USA one will find millions of Americans who were worse off than him. I just could not help thinking about his motives being rooted in aversion against Latinos. But the media obviously did not want to touch upon this controversial subject. A considerable segment of the Anglo American population looked askance at persons of Latin American descent. Their arguments were that Latinos were dishonest and unclean. I personally never shared those beliefs and interpreted these arguments as unfounded prejudices of the ignorant. Many Latinos merely worked in "dirty jobs", like sanitation and agriculture. Yet Anglo Americans do not always welcome persons of even slightly different cultures, but that does not usually lead to mass homicide.

A number of Latin Americans kept entering the USA over the "green border" and San Martino was heavily frequented in that respect. I got to see those small groups of men, sometimes women among them, running across the roads and hiding in bushes and ditches. They would then suddenly and frantically board an approaching automobile and disappear as quickly as they came. The US Border Patrol was present all over this small town and eager to catch these people, to bring them back to the border gate, from where they often returned within less than a day. Nonetheless the area of San Alberto was not the destination of those migrants. Most of them intended to travel further north to Los Angeles or San Francisco and the international boundary was only the first obstacle on their adventurous journey. The US border patrol maintained checkpoints on most major freeways, approximately forty miles north of the Mexican border and this stretch of their voyage was usually travelled in the trunk of a car. They were called "Brazero's" in the old days, and also "Wetbacks", since in many regions the border between the USA and Mexico is divided by rivers, which must be crossed in order to reach the neighbouring nation incognito. Most of these people were farm labourers who brought in the harvest between late spring and fall. Thereafter they usually returned to Latin America for the winter.

The Hispanic population of the USA referred to the paperless migrants as "Pollo's", which means chickens and to those aiding their traveling endeavours within this country as "Pollero's" a Spanish word for chicken farmer or chicken dealer. I repeatedly observed indications that two of my neighbours at the motel where I resided appeared to be engaged in that clandestine line of commerce, but, of course, I kept looking the other way. A man's business is his business.

The time came to part with my aging station wagon. The tags on its license plates were about to expire and based upon my situation I was unable to renew the registration. Driving around with an expired plate meant risking getting stopped by the police and that was exactly what I had to avoid in those days.

Station wagons were in demand across the border to be restored as taxi cabs and it took little time to find a buyer for the vehicle. Afterwards I had to find a replacement. A large sedan was offered for sale in the newspaper. It was in good condition and its plates were valid for almost a year. I did not hesitate to buy it. The searchlight on the front of the driver's door, the small hubcaps and the two antennas on its trunk left no doubts about the official origin of the unmarked police car. When I returned to the motel I parked the vehicle near my quarters and slowly walked up the stairs.

As I passed by my neighbour's room, I realized his door was ajar. Then I heard somebody hissing the word 'Fuzz!' – An expression for police in American street jargon.

'Where?' I returned.

'Are you blind man?' the voice continued, 'There is a cop car parked downstairs.'

'I am sorry,' I replied almost embarrassed, 'that's only my private set of wheels, I just bought it.' 'Oh man, your Dakota license plate looks at first glance like one from the federal government, and so does your damned car! I thought we were all in for a raid!'

Meanwhile my other neighbour stepped outside his room. 'You seem to be stirring up some apprehension with your vehicle around here,' he said with a broad smile, as he stuck out his hand in my direction. 'Arturo's the name.' 'Harry.' I shook his hand. 'Pleased to meet you Arturo.' 'Xavier,' his neighbour introduced himself. 'Let's go inside, I need a beer after this shock,' he suggested. 'Let's have a toast to good old times when we had a better life,' Arturo said as we sat down, with a beer in our hands. 'Right you are, let's drink to that,' I agreed with a painful, sarcastic smile on my face. Arturo's expression turned pensive and earnest. I realized immediately that I was not the only one who had seen better times. Xavier and I did not say a word, just as if we expected Arturo to continue with an explanation for his sudden mood change. And he did.

'Not that long ago I had my own house, my wife, my children and a good job,' he started, 'but one day a hoodlum committed a robbery in the vicinity where I lived. Unfortunately he drove an automobile resembling my own car like a twin brother. I was driving homewards when my vehicle got wedged in by two police cars. My children got yanked from the back seat and I was first tossed to the floor, and then into jail.' He remained silent for a moment then I asked, 'Did they ever apologize, were you paid an award for damages?' 'Oh, I got an award alright,' he said, 'the police planted illegal drugs in my car to 'justify' the violent, false arrest. I served a pretty good jail sentence, lost my job and my house. My wife gave me the walking papers. So here I am, working in a trade where no references are required.'

After a moment of silence I decided to narrate the experience I gathered in California during the past five years. When I was done, my neighbours looked at me with an expression as if I had told them that the Russians were coming or the Martians had landed. I changed the subject and continued with a controversial question. 'These people who cross the border illegally – can't they get a visa to work here seasonally to bring in the harvest?' My neighbours shrugged. 'We just bring them where they want to go, we don't ask questions,' was Xavier's reply. Questions were obviously unwelcome in this world I was about to enter, and confidence a kind of scarce commodity.

Shortly thereafter, I acquired a false US birth certificate. My name was henceforth Harrison, (Harry) Josef Burger. I 'became' the son of a European immigrant couple, born in the USA, but raised in Europe, which would account for my slight accent. I still continued my relentless efforts to obtain support from the government. Among those was a request I directed at a California State Senator, and I got an answer.

Dear (Sir)

Thank you for your recent correspondence regarding the obstruction of due process of law.

Because I do not represent the area in which you reside, legislative courtesy requires that I forward your correspondence to Senator W. D. I know he will be most interested in your views and will do what ever is appropriate.

Sincerely, W.C. State Senator, California

I was not about to get my hopes up about receiving help from a politician for a change. And I was right. What was 'appropriate' read like this;

Dear (Sir)

Senator C. has forwarded your letter to me for reply. Regrettably I can only suggest that you contact the District Attorney who may be able to help you, for as a Legislator, I can help make the laws but I cannot enforce them.

If you have other concerns regarding state matters, please write again.

Very truly yours, W. D. State Senator, California

A Hispanic gentleman by the moniker "Gordo" showed up occasionally at the motel. He seemed to be engaged in the same trade as both of my neighbours, and one morning he kept walking back and forth in the rear parking lot. I coincidentally passed by and spotted a number of shoe tips sticking out from thick shrubbery at the fence, dividing the motel property from the freeway exit. I had only exchanged a few words with Gordo, but he seemed to trust me. 'Good heavens,' he said nervously, 'Every time I need a driver there is none around! These people need to go to the stash house in San Alberto right away.'

'How much?' was my short reply. 'Two hundred dollars.' I stuck up my thumb and opened the trunk of my car. I had been told how much money I would get, but not how many people I had to drive. Half a village, it seemed, emerged from the bushes. After the trunk was full a number of people streamed into the passenger compartment, where they crouched down to remain invisible. I jumped behind the steering wheel, and followed Gordo's car.

My rear bumper scratched the motel driveway as I pulled out on the street. Unscathed we reached our destination. 'Would you perhaps be interested in driving my second automobile with some people to Los Angeles tomorrow?' Gordo queried, as he handed me the amount agreed upon.

'I'll be happy to.' I answered.

Shortly after seven o'clock the subsequent morning Gordo knocked on my door. 'Are you ready to go to work?'

'You bet!' In a suit and tie, I opened the driver's door of the big, late model sedan, started the motor and turned into the freeway. I realized that the vehicle had been professionally adapted for the job. The rear suspension was reinforced and the car was pleasant to drive. The only aspect that did not fit into the picture was me. My entire life had so far been marked by law obedience and legitimacy. Illicit activities were foreign to me. But America had confronted me with its peculiarities and I needed to adapt to the situation. After all who would hire a driver without a working permit and without a driver's license, except a Pollero?

As I reached the city of San Alberto, the traffic was beginning to increase and that worked to my advantage. Often the border patrol shut down the checkpoint to avoid miles of traffic jams. I hoped that this would be the case as I approached the area. But I was mistaken; yellow flashlights were blinking at both sides of the road, and a sign was lit with the words "US Border Patrol, all vehicles must stop." So I needed something that would divert the attention of the agents away from me, and spotted a couple of casually dressed black gentlemen in an aging, dented van in front of me. I stepped on the gas and positioned myself in front of their automobile. As I got closer to the agent I looked calmly over the hood of the car as my palms started to get moist. The officer promptly kept looking at the van he was about to stop and check and waved me through.

Gordo had observed my passage from his car a slight distance behind me. Then he passed me on the left before his right turn signal began to flash near a freeway exit and I followed him behind an old factory, where we traded vehicles hastily. 'Your money is on the driver's seat. I'll pick up the car at the motel tomorrow,' Gordo said as he jumped into the sedan, and both of us left the area without delay. The three hundred dollars on top of the seat were more than welcome to me. The funds from the sale of my travel trailer were dwindling and I had to keep myself from starving. But I made these trips only occasionally, since this type of activity was an inordinately high risk for somebody in my position.

Restrained economic aspects caused me to look around for an even less expensive place to live. I found it a few hundred meters north of the border on San Martino Boulevard. The "Toreador" was a stately motel built in the thirties. Its white buildings and partition walls were covered with red tiles. Little flowerbeds and a grass strip separated the approximately thirty meters long building from the sidewalk. In its centre, a majestic double door made of dark wood led into the spacious lobby. The reception hall, about five meters tall, had a door to the right behind the entrance where a good sized bar accommodated over fifty guests. To the left, a passage adorned with stylish ironwork opened into the restaurant. To the opposite of the entrance a broad staircase connected the main floor with a u-shaped gallery above, where the apartments and rooms for the personnel were located.

Mural paintings adorned the pleasant atmosphere of the interior, complemented by the huge red carpet covering the entire lobby. A door to the right of the stairs led to the large swimming pool in the back of the building, with its bottom showing a large mosaic of a bullfighter in action. The one story buildings for the motel guests stood in a half circle around the central edifice and it's fenced off pool, with ample parking spaces between. A two-story apartment building to the north and an additional parking lot with a small laundry house to the south surrounded the four acre property.

Upon closer look, the handsome place appeared rather sordid. The pool was empty and the restaurant and bar were closed down. The motel rooms were rented out only by the month. Obviously, the Toreador had seen better days. Its numerous palm trees used to be lit with coloured spotlights at night, antique carriages embellished the triangle shaped green spots between the two double entrance driveways and charming little fountains were burbling besides it. Comedian Buster Keaton's brother tended the bar, where celebrities like John Wayne had stepped in for a drink. Sometimes there were even fashion-shows presented in the main building.

'These good old days are gone,' Rafael, the innkeeper said wistfully. 'The current owners have no money for a renovation.' The Mexican-American gentleman had been managing the Toreador already for over a decade. The guest list consisted of mostly welfare recipients, retirees, a few Pollero's as well as now and then some characters who seemed to be have been touched by the Great Spirit. Some of them might have been wondering about my pulling in with large, late model cars during the subsequent months, but people around here pretty much minded their own business and I was glad for having found a roof over my head for two hundred dollars a month.

CHAPTER SIX

Pollero's were a tight lipped society, suspecting almost everybody to be a police informer. Gordo's business partner by the name of Isaac was no exception in that respect. He always met me with a polite reluctance. Some days he must have been unable to find a driver, and had little choice but to knock on my door. This time I had to collect the passengers in San Martino. It was late in the evening and it was beginning to get dark when I stopped at the various locations, always on guard for the countless border patrol vehicles cruising around the village.

Nobody was following me with a second car to the Los Angeles area. Instead I was provided with an address to deliver the migrants. Fortunately the checkpoint was closed. I had no difficulty in finding the house being the supposed destination, but the place was dark and nobody was home. Isaac gave me the phone number of his home, where I could reach his wife in case of problems. So I quickly drove off, looking for a phone booth.

Only half a mile down the road a large supermarket with a big parking lot and payphones mounted on the wall came in sight, but the store was open. I needed a more discrete location to stop. If passers-by heard voices coming from the trunk of the parked vehicle, or if those in the car began rocking it with nobody in the passenger compartment, things could get out of hand. Around two miles further ahead I got to a smaller commercial centre stretching about five hundred meters along the street, so I pulled into the endless long parking lot after I spotted a phone booth. It was ten o'clock in the evening and relatively quiet in this south eastern suburb of Los Angeles. There was hardly any traffic on the four lane street, only one or two cars passed by every minute. Somewhere in the distance I heard a dog barking and an aging transformer was humming on a telephone pole.

I had just begun to dial the phone number when a large sedan slowly turned into the parking lot approximately one hundred meters away. What I did not like about the vehicle was its roof line. Nobody would mount ski carriers in the summertime. The car's headlights were shining at me and my parked automobile. So I hung up the phone and walked towards the approaching patrol vehicle.

'Good evening officer,' I started the conversation, 'I'm lost; could you tell me how to get to first -street in Westminster?'

'Good evening Sir,' the policeman replied politely, 'Go back here to the left, 'til the freeway entrance north, from there it's about five miles to the exit.'

'Unit twenty one,' a voice from his two way radio cawed.

'Two one roger,' the officer responded.

'Five o two suspect, northbound on Victoria, near Brookhearst!'

'Two one roger; on the way!'

'Drive carefully,' the officer said with his head turned into my direction, before the red and blue lights on his roof began to flash, and his siren awoke the neighbourhood, as the patrol car shot out into the street. Five – o – two corresponded to drunk driver. I was not really fond of those individuals, but this one came like a blessing in disguise. Quickly I left the area and drove off until I found another public phone, from where I called Isaac's wife.

Pollero's tend to work somewhat sloppy, I concluded. Sloppiness does not bode well with illicit activities. In the following week I was on my way to Los Angeles again. In this instance I did not have to collect the migrants, but instead to distribute them around L.A. North of the checkpoint I let them out of the trunk and into the passenger compartment. I just could not let them stay cooped up like sardines for several hours. Dusk was fortunately about to fall. A well dressed gringo and five Latinos looking somewhat grubby after their unorthodox crossing of the border just don't look right sitting in the same automobile. The typical Los Angeles smog lay in the warm evening air, as I was on my way to bring the last one of my passengers to Santa Ana. Police cars were patrolling all over town, until I got closer to our destination.

An eerie silence and darkness began to surround us. The three story buildings were of recent make, but there was hardly any traffic on the streets. Scants of smashed street lights were laying in the gullies. The little district appeared about as safe as a minefield and whoever was hanging around these sidewalks at night left the impression of having an extensive record of previous criminal convictions about as long as the Santa Monica Boulevard.

After I parked the car, we opened the doors and got out. A suspicious, young Latino stood only a few meters away from us. 'Hola!' he greeted us in a sing song voice. He was looking at me, holding a slender joint between his fingers. 'Hola que onda!' I returned in Central American Street jargon. Anglo Americans were about as welcome around here as dead flies floating in your breakfast coffee. The marihuana smoker must have been satisfied with my reply in Spanish and must have reckoned that I was a Latino myself. At night all cats look black. With an uneasy feeling in the pit of my stomach I followed my passenger by the name of Fernando across the street.

We climbed up a couple of flights of stairs, where Fernando knocked in a particular rhythm on an apartment door. A stunningly beautiful Latina opened. 'Fernando!' she greeted the man joyfully and somewhat surprised. Then she looked at me as if she did not know what to make of this tall gringo in a suit and tie. 'Me trajo este Señor,' Fernando tried to explain my presence. The lady seemed relieved that I was not some type of public official; she turned around and got her purse. 'Here is the money for the passage Señor,' she said. Accompanied by the friendly words, 'buenas noches,' she closed the door.

I turned around and walked down the stairs. When I was about to leave the building I looked around carefully. This was the kind of American neighbourhood where a fortyfour magnum in one hand and a bad mannered Rottweiler dog on the other seemed mandatory to walk around. I was delighted to see the interior lights in my car turning on as I opened its door. So the car battery had not been stolen yet. I did not waste any time to get to the next freeway and out of this concrete jungle.

As I rolled southward I realized that this type of work was

too high a risk for somebody in my position. I had to advise Gordo and Isaac that I henceforth would only accept driving vehicles with the migrants already in the trunk to not more than one place north of the checkpoint. That seemed to mark the end of my career as a Pollero assistant. There were always plenty of penniless folks around the vicinity not afraid to risk replacing me, and soon after I found myself standing there with an empty wallet.

Wrapped up in my thoughts, I stood in the front yard of the Toreador watching the traffic on the street going by, as a voice behind me said, 'How are you doing?'

'Could be worse I suppose, the rent is due and I am broke!' was my answer. 'You too?'

'Right on!' Jeff was an Anglo American in his thirties. He had moved to the Toreador recently and appeared to be making a living the same way I did. 'I know where I can pick up five hundred dollars right now, but I don't have a car,' he continued.

'If that's all that's holding you up, there is mine. I just don't have any gas and no money to buy some.'

'Let's go fifty- fifty,' Jeff suggested.

'Sounds great but where's the money?'

'Northeast of Los Angeles; can you make it about ten miles? My ex-wife will lend me a twenty!'

It was early afternoon when we passed by the checkpoint of the inland freeway near Escondera. 'It always feels like money lost driving through these places with an empty trunk, doesn't it?' Jeff remarked. 'Unfortunately this car is my entire net worth right now, so I can't consider that option,' I returned cynically.

It was a long commute and as we began to approach our destination the last glow of sundown disappeared on the western horizon. We had to leave the freeway and continued on a broad two lane country road. It was one of those typical western US highways surrounded by rolling hills with brown, dry grass bushels on mostly barren grounds. I switched on the headlights as darkness began to surround us. Miles ahead the dim lights of a distant, small township became visible. Then Jeff told me to slow down. 'In about a mile we must take a left,' he said, but I could see nothing of our supposed destination. 'Here, turn left,' Jeff directed me into a narrow field path. Very slowly I made my way down the rocky driveway, 'Pretty soon we'll need a jeep to continue.' The terrain was getting me concerned for the state of the car. 'Just stop and turn off the engine, we're here,' in what seemed to be the middle of nowhere.

'We are – where? There is nothing but field mice, rabbits and rattlesnakes in this vicinity,' I concluded. 'Just wait and see,' Jeff grinned. I opened my car door and stepped outside. Now I recognized what appeared to be thousands of orange trees, neatly planted in symmetrical lines all the way to a mountain in the background. I started to ask myself if we drove all these miles to steal oranges.

It was pitch dark and as quiet as a cemetery. The moonlight was shining on the peaks of the mountain and the crowns of the little trees looked almost like an army of soldiers about to take on the dark giant hill with its silver lining towering above them. Suddenly I heard voices coming closer. Jeff seemed to appear out of nowhere with a couple of farm labourers flanking him. 'I just told them, that you were a corrupt official whom I must pay a bribe,' he said with a broad smile. 'If they didn't believe me they could come and see the patrol car.' I came to realize that I hadn't laughed during the past four years, but a grin and a chuckle came over my face as I said, 'You seem to know your business!'

'Well, these guys still owe me five hundred from my last trip.' Jeff explained, before he told me to come along. So I followed the little group into the trees until tall brush seemed to end our path. A worker pushed the shrubbery aside, and a wooden building, about twelve meters long became visible. A feeble little light bulb threw its discrete shimmer on a small porch, where a couple of cats seemed to be waiting for mice to chase. A lady stepped out the door and brought a couple of chairs. 'Siente se Señores!' she said with a friendly smile. Suddenly a car engine started closing in and I instinctively turned my head in the direction the noise was coming from. 'El Compadre, Señor, he is going to bring your money,' the woman explained.

'Feels like a million dollars!' Jeff frolicked as we sat back in the car.

'Right you are,' I concluded, 'these days a one hundred dollar bill looks as big as a bedspread.' As I slowed down and activated the turn signal to roll into the parking lot of the first hamburger joint on the road, Jeff reflected, 'This must have been E.S.P.!'

'To hell with the E.S.P. – it's my growling stomach!' I replied.

With a broad smile of relief, I put two one hundred dollar bills on Rafael's reception desk the following morning. 'A little bit late, I am sorry for that,' I added sheepishly. Rafael put his hands over the two bank bills with a friendly smile. Then he slowly pushed the money back into my direction. 'You have helped me quite a bit around here by attending the lobby in the past weeks. I'll tell you what we are going to do. You can continue giving me a hand around here for a few hours a day and you can keep your room for free.'

'That sounds great, much obliged sir.' I was relieved, to say the least, that I had managed to stumble across a legitimate means of income. This offer came like a gift from heaven. I had a roof over my head, now I just needed to find a means to make some money during the time I was not needed in the motel, to keep me from starving.

Meanwhile the plates on my current automobile were about to expire, so I had to sell. I succeeded in getting a decent price. During the following days, I managed to barter down the price on two large sedans for sale in San Alberto. 'Are you starting a used car lot?' Rafael asked jokingly as I drove in with the second vehicle. 'I wish I could,' I returned, 'but if each one of those two makes me one hundred and fifty dollars profit I am satisfied.' And they did – in less than three weeks.

Reading the used car ads in the regional newspaper became a regular habit for me. Soon I averaged around three hundred dollars per month buying and selling used cars. It was an income far away from a comfortable means of living, but a lot for somebody in my position. Asides from attending the motel desk and selling cars, I continued my efforts addressing about every imaginable level of government. Now and then I got a reply, like this one:

Dear (Sir)

Thank you for contacting Congressman B. L.'s office with your concerns.

Because you do not reside in the 41'st Congressional District, and in keeping with long-standing Congressional courtesy you may wish to contact D. H. However, your problems do not appear to involve the Federal Government. You may desire to seek remedy by pursuing your case through private and professional legal action.

Once again, thank you for your request. I hope this information is helpful to you.

Sincerely, C. S. Field Representative for Congressman B. L.

The congressman I was referred to in this letter I had contacted already, but I had never received an answer. In the meantime my consulate must have realized beyond any doubt that their office had been misinformed by the City of Escondera, pertinent to my suit against that community. But it seemed that our diplomats appeared to be satisfied with the situation.

My firm belief, that the USA was a democratic state of rights, comparable with my homeland, was obviously the mistake of my life. Counting upon my country's readiness to intervene on behalf of their citizens abroad, appeared to be the second biggest error I've ever committed. The effect of both led to consequences most Europeans simply could not anticipate; not within a large, industrialized, modern nation, built mostly by European immigrants, and definitely not as a direct subject of a friendship treaty.

In my part time job as a reception clerk, I gradually got to know the tenants of the complex. Most of them were polite Hispanic and Anglo American folks. Among them was a gentleman by the name of Bob Nellis. He was well into his sixties and had worked most of his life as a baker on a huge US military troop transporting ship. The sociable southerner from Alabama lived off a decent monthly pension, but that money did not seem to last very long. The issue was not so much his thirsty soul, yearning for beer by the case on a daily basis, but his passion to bet on racehorses. At the first of the month he paid his rent, put some money aside for his nutrition, and went straight to the racetrack, usually across the border. Every time, like clockwork, he came back flat broke as well as slightly tipsy. He wouldn't really stagger, but seemed to walk partly sideways, almost like a crab. This unusual marching style was complemented by his raised right hand with the forefinger waving back and forth, probably a tardy form of self reproach. But San Martino was nothing short of blessed with people referred to as strange birds, and the Latin population always seemed to see the humour in human imperfection.

It was not yet the first of the month when Bob entered the lobby, but he had those pages of the regional newspapers already under his arm, containing all the schedules for the horse races and he seemed to be in a hurry. 'I need one hundred dollars. I got an I.O.U. made out for one hundred fifty to be paid at the first of the coming month!' I took the bill from my wallet. Bob grasped for it like a fish for a worm. 'Five dollars for a ride to the border?' were his subsequent words. I did not want to pass on that opportunity either. When I returned Rafael smiled while shaking his head. 'I am afraid this character is merely getting older, but if he wants to throw his money away, you can use it the most.' Bob became a regular and appreciated customer of mine. And occasionally my total monthly income came close to that of the minimal wage prescribed in this country.

A gentleman of south-western European descent had moved into the Toreador. He was a particularly friendly man in his forties. When I exchanged a few words with him, he shared with me his experience of being discriminated against by the regional legal system, just as I had been. However due to his modest articulacy in the English language I was unable to understand the details of his circumstances. But he was also a foreigner, who could have been affected by curtailments of human rights for aliens; if the according statement from that lawyer I received a couple of years ago was correct.

Another new tenant who arrived here recently was Tom. The tall and brawny Hispanic gentleman from New Mexico was just as fluent in English as in Spanish. He was well educated, always well dressed, and had good manners. An amnesty for illegal aliens was under way, and Tom sensed an opportunity for business as an immigration consultant in the region.

For quite some time I was wondering about the exact contents of this ominous treaty between my home country and the USA. In the central public library in San Alberto I finally found it.

CONVENTION OF FRIENDSHIP, COMMERCE, AND EXTRADITION

ARTICLE 1

The citizens of the United States of America and those of (my home country) shall be admitted and treated upon a footing of reciprocal equality in the two countries, where such admission and treatment shall not conflict with the constitutional or legal previsions, as well federal as state and (provincial) of the contracting parties.

The citizens of the United States and the citizens of (my home country) as well as the members of their families, subject to the constitutional and legal provisions aforesaid, and yielding obedience to the laws, regulations, and usages of the country wherein they reside, shall be at liberty to come, go, sojourn temporarily, domiciliate or establish themselves permanently, the former in the (provinces of my home country) the (citizens of my home country) in the states of the American Union, to acquire, possess and alienate therein property, to manage their affairs; to exercise their professions, their industry, and their commerce; to have establishments; to possess warehouses; to consign their products and their merchandise, and sell them by wholesale or retail, either by themselves or such brokers or other agents as they may think proper; they shall have free access to the tribunals, and shall be at liberty to prosecute and defend their rights before courts of justice in the same manner as native citizens, either by themselves or by such advocates, attorneys, or other agents as they may think proper to select.

No pecuniary or other more burdensome conditions shall be imposed upon their residence or establishments, or upon the enjoyment of the above mentioned rights, than shall be imposed upon citizens of the country where they reside, nor any condition whatever to which the latter shall not be subject.

The foregoing privileges, however, shall not extend to the exercise of political rights, nor to participation in the property of communities, corporations or institutions of which the citizens of one party, established in the other, shall not have become members or co-proprietors.

It appeared that similar treaties entered between the USA and dozens of other countries on every continent were currently in force, at least on paper, but not necessarily in practice, as the following reader contribution to a newspaper indicated:

EVEN NONCITIZENS HERE LEGALLY SHOULD BE WARY OF POLICE

James G. (Opinion, Nov.21) makes the comment that "the rights and privileges of the Constitution are not reserved exclusively for citizens. Noncitizens are protected by the Bill of Rights and other amendments as surely as descendants of pilgrim families."

This is a nice sentiment and may be the law, but it is not what is practiced on the street.

I am a (foreign) citizen here legally, and I have had a good deal of trouble with the police in Southern California, although I have as yet to be convicted of as much as illegal parking.

I have had guns put to my head by the police, have been told by the police that "Noncitizens have no rights" and was told by a Border Patrol agent at the checkpoint on Interstate 15: "I am the law. I own every street in every county in every state in this country. (The US-) President told me so."

I have learned to carry no more money on me than absolutely necessary; not to transport or possess in a public place any property which I would really care to have confiscated; to take great pains to avoid law enforcement agents; and to never let them have my right address.

If noncitizens have rights in fact and not simply in theory, the police should be notified of this, and they should be instructed that they enforce the law, that they are not the law.

A. Johnson, "San Alberto"

Under the conditions mentioned in this letter not even the biggest foreign corporations would have any certainty of rights. As a matter of fact, rights could no longer even be obtained by hiring top notch lawyers, because there simply would not be any rights. Foreign tourists were better protected under prevailing laws of threshold countries, and the USA would add an entirely new dimension to the meaning of the term "High Risk Venture Capital" for foreign investments in their country.

The gentleman who entered the lobby one afternoon was about forty years old. He was slender and his hair seemed to be greying prematurely. The tall Anglo American was well spoken, courteous and modest. 'Would you happen to have a room for rent by the month?' he asked politely.

'Yes sir, we do,' I replied. 'Number eight is ready, if you'd like to take at look at it; it's to your left, right around the corner.' I handed him the key.

'Thank you, I will be right back,' he answered as he left the lobby through the back door. He did not appear to be a typical American, I thought perhaps a Canadian? When he returned about five minutes later he had already put his belongings in his room. He handed me the money for the rent. 'This used to be a really beautiful place, why is everything slowly dilapidating here?'

'The owners don't seem to have the funds for a renovation, so it is slowly going down hill.' He shook his head, 'Capitalist throw away society!'

This type of comment was unusual in America and I made a somewhat daring remark: 'Are you a leftist?' I asked with a smile.

'Let's say perhaps left of this system.'

'Well, I suppose I cannot hold that against anybody in this society,' I returned pensively.

'I don't hear that too often, it sounds as if your life aint exactly the American dream, in our land of opportunity.'

'You can say that again,' I nodded my head. 'Are you a US American?'

'Born and raised, but not always with all my heart and soul. And where are you from?'

'Europe.'

'How long have you been working here?'

'About a year, but only part time.'

'And the rest of the time?'

'I buy and sell used cars.'

'So you're an innkeeper and a salesman.'

'Unfortunately that is all I've been left with.'

'How do you mean?'

'Oh, that is a long story. I don't think you want to hear it.'

'I got time, and time is all I got. By the way my name is Sam,' the friendly stranger stuck out his hand. 'Harry' I returned, 'Pleased to meet you Sam!'

The narration of my past seven years in the USA took about five minutes. When I was done, Sam looked thunderstruck. 'I have heard a number of incredible stories, but this one really takes the cake!' he said.

'I've got dozens of documents supporting my contentions, I'd be glad to get those so you can look at them.'

'No, I believe you, that's not what surprises me. But an official agency in the United States lying to a foreign diplomat of a country with whom we enjoy a century old friendship, – that is really brazen! Have you informed state and federal governments about this?' A rather painful, sarcastic smile must have come over my face as I replied, 'what do you think I've been doing for more than half a decade? I've been phoning, visiting and writing to just about every imaginable public office in this nation, but if I do get a reply, which is rather the exception than the rule, it is a rejection.'

Sam shook his head. 'My goodness, this is incredible. Have you also addressed our politicians?' 'You bet, I already have a little collection of their replies to my correspondence; 'Sorry for being unable to assist you...'

'How about your embassy?'

'It appears that only a few diplomatic interventions seem possible within a year. Ordinary countries are very reluctant to risk political friction with a superpower. If average citizens face shortcomings in a banana republic, they might get help from diplomats. But in a country as big and mighty as this one, assistance from the diplomatic side is rather reserved for very important persons.'

'Why were you and Sullivan never charged, and summoned to a court of law for all those wrongdoings you were being accused of?'

'Those alleged wrongdoings of ours were nothing but an orchestrated libel, slander and innuendo campaign. It would be exposed as exactly that in the course of an impartial investigation, that's why.'

'Why don't you file the suit again?'

'Meanwhile my visa has expired, and under the circumstances it is not prudent for me to try and have it renewed. Cassell threatened to incriminate me at the immigration and naturalization service. Asides from that, the City of Escondera could start another attack against the both of us.'

'You're right; you seem to be sitting in a trap. But have you ever explained your case to the media?'

'After Sullivan made innumerable fruitless attempts to try and get attention from the press and TV, I made a number of tries myself, but also without success.'

'Where is Gale Cassell now?' Sam wanted to know.

'From what I last heard, he was working for a couple of Italian American Brothers.'

'Here in California?'

'No, those two were at that time in Chicago.'

'And they're not there anymore?'

'According to the media, they ended up under a ranch somewhere in the Midwest.'

'On a ranch?'

'No, beneath it. That's where the FBI recently dug up what was left of them.'

'Jesus Christ!' was Sam's reaction.

'What amazes me is that you are not getting any help from our system," Sam was in disbelief. 'Our civil population is an entirely different matter.'

'I have meanwhile realized that, but how come?'

'Didn't it occur to you that something is not right with most of our people over here?'

'Not really, Americans appeared to me as courteous friendly folk during my first visits, but what do you really mean?'

'Most of us don't mean what we say, and we don't say what we mean. People are not actually real, – they seem to act their way through life by means of pretence. We are not the most honest, courteous and friendliest society on the face of this earth.

'Less than one hundred years ago, the American west was a very sparsely populated, wide open country. Almost everybody was allowed to annex land just about as they pleased. In that aspect we were not very considerate with the natives either. It was an every man for himself attitude ruling life around here. In the meantime the west has been settled, nobody is allowed to grab and run as in the old days. But many of us have not really grown out of this wild romantic epoch yet. Their prerogative seems to be: What can I get away with unpunished, instead of leading a life by respecting other people's rights. 'On the other hand, our first settlements on the east coast were established in the early seventeenth century. The prevailing customs, rules and laws of ancient Europe became the foundation of America. If you examine history, you will realize that your home continent was still torturing heretics to death, and burning witches at the stake in those years.

'America subsequently developed independent from Europe for centuries. The dark ages of Europe were rather a transient occurrence within your continent. But the medieval European heritage is part of the very foundation that this country was built upon. We need more time to rid ourselves of this mind-set. Nowadays, Europeans obviously consider Americans to be prude, superstitious and cantankerous, for merely being ancient European. Thirdly this country happens to be culturally cast by people of European descent. But we do not enjoy the harmonious atmosphere among mere traditional inhabitants, as in a European nation. Our population is comprised of numerous cultures and races. The individual US American cannot easily identify himself with the broader public. As a consequence, our population is almost fragmentized into various groups, becoming increasingly jealous of each other, and occasionally selfish and inconsiderate if not to say ruthless. We have become individualistic, and our patriotism is focusing increasingly upon our territory instead of the people.

'Consequently our concern about any forms of wrongdoing remains within bounds, as long as we are not personally affected by it. We are taught not to think in terms of 'what goes around – comes around'. Any form of social-political collectivism is met with reluctance over here, we are very wary of what ever might taste of socialism.' Sam concluded. And I had just received a great deal of insight into American society, which was becoming increasingly foreign to me, the longer I lived among it. Right along with many Europeans, I seemed to have misjudged America entirely. Or had this country turned for the worse within the past decade? That was probably not a question of one *or* the other, but an issue of one *and* the other.

'May I ask you a personal question?' Sam said after a long moment of silence.

'Yes of course.'

'Have you ever been involved in organized or serious criminal activities in your life?' A friendly smile appeared on my face. 'Believe it or not, since my childhood I've belonged to those strange birds who believe in law and order; this was the way I'd been brought up. To avoid starvation I drove some illegal aliens up to L. A. and I am currently selling used cars without a dealer's license. But asides from that, I've only been fined over occasional traffic infractions, over here as well as back home, otherwise I've never been into trouble with the law.'

'I contemplated that you could possibly be a criminal, so our system would deny you protection as a victim.'

'No, I am not a crook, much less a matricide killer as I was made out to be, and those accusations may be only the tip of the iceberg.' I concluded with a fatalistic tone in my voice. 'Good heavens.' Sam returned, 'You must continue to address your plight to our politicians. There are plenty of decent people within our government who will not tolerate this mess you were put in.'

CHAPTER SEVEN

Tom had meanwhile opened his immigration office, and I contemplated becoming one of his first clients. But my inquiries into the matter received a rather distressing reply. At that particular time, when I would have needed to be present illegally in this country, was unfortunately shortly before my visa expired. Therewith I could not qualify under this proviso. But this was merely yet another disappointment of many I had to get use to in all those years. I had to be glad for having a roof over my head and something to eat.

Once in a while I prepared a hearty meal in the kitchen of the shut down restaurant within the main building. One day I was doing exactly that, as Rafael shouted my name. 'The county grand jury is on the phone asking for you,' he said somewhat excited. Needless to say, that I left the food in the pans, and virtually ran to the phone. After John Sullivan had unsuccessfully attempted to get the attention of this government agency, I kept trying to get a reply from them on an annual basis. Now I had obviously succeeded. 'We would like to discuss your complaint to the grand jury with you. Could you come to our office this coming Friday at ten thirty a.m.?'

'Yes madam,' I replied, 'I will be at your place punctually.' Sam had coincidently stepped into the lobby, and witnessed my phone call. 'I knew it,' he said with a smile on his face, 'now everything is going to work out for you!' But I was not that confident. I had already had so many contacts with public agencies in these matters, but in the end those amounted to nothing and I was eventually turned away.

As agreed I appeared at the offices of the grand jury in time. I was led into a barren conference room with about ten chairs and two large tables. A gentleman and a lady introduced themselves to me; Mr. Bolt and Mrs. James. Both were well dressed and in their fifties. Mr. Bolt politely opened the discussion.

'We have contacted the City of Escondera about your complaint, but nobody there appears to know anything about you or what you are alleging. What really happened here?'

'Our business entered into a joint venture agreement to assist a transportation company in their subchapter-11 reorganization. During this relationship a series of criminal offenses, including theft, fraud, embezzlement and conversion were committed to our detriment. Subsequently our company was burglarized three times. We were gradually deprived of vehicles, records, equipment and so forth. The police in jurisdiction initially refused to respond. After they eventually did, we were denied police reports. Subsequently our manager was arrested when he announced his according law suit against that city. Finally my consul was being misled by officials of this city.'

'Were the perpetrators ever arrested?' Mrs. James wanted to know. 'I am afraid not, it appears that members of the Escondera police department supported them to some extent.'

'What? This is really strange!' Mrs. James concluded. 'Have you ever contacted the federal grand jury in this matter? It looks as if some aspects might fall under their jurisdiction,' Mr. Bolt asked me. 'Yes sir I have, but I never got a reply.'

'Never mind,' Mr. Bolt returned, 'We might contact them accordingly.'

'You will hear from us,' Mrs. James assured me, as she led me to the door.

'Thank you very much,' I said and nodded politely before I left the room.

I was by no means confident that the long awaited turn-around of my life was right ahead of me, but I felt some hope nonetheless. It was after all the first time an official agency invited me for a discussion of these matters, after I'd contacted over one hundred government offices without success. When I got back to San Martino, I asked Tom about the exact nature and duties of a grand jury. 'A grand jury primarily investigates cases of improprieties within the government system, and it operates in the case of a county grand jury under the supervision of the district attorney,' Tom advised me. This reply was anything but uplifting considering my past experiences with the district attorney's office. After John Sullivan unsuccessfully tried to get help from the district attorney's offices, I did so myself, in person, by phone and numerous times by mail. My latest correspondence to the D.A. went by registered mail, but without any response whatsoever!

A younger gentleman who had moved into the Toreador about that time was a Hispanic around twenty-five years old. He seemed to be a recently landed South American immigrant, by the name of Cesar Alvarez. One morning, after I was done with sorting out the mail for the tenants, Cesar staggered into the lobby. 'Somebody just hit me over the head,' he told me, clearly traumatised. He almost made it to the reception desk when he collapsed. I dialled 911 on the telephone, the nationwide emergency number for police, fire service and medical rescue. 'The rescue and ambulance units are on their way!' I was told.

I got a woollen blanket to cover him, put a glass of water beside him, and asked him to put his ID on his chest, in case he lost consciousness. 911 is a great concept for emergency calls, but it is monitored by police. Only two minutes after I hung up the phone, a male and a female officer from the San Alberto police entered the lobby. The policeman made some derogatory comment about the patient when he came in the door. Subsequently he addressed the injured man by his first name. 'You can call 911 and tell them to call back the rescue units; the county can not always incur costs for these people.' The officer shouted in my direction. For a moment I could not believe my eyes and ears. 'I am sorry officer, but this person is obviously hurt!' I replied. The constable grabbed his walky-talky and called off the ambulance. 'He can call a private ambulance if he thinks he needs one,' he barked as he left the lobby. The lady officer did not say a single word during her entire presence, but I could sense that she did not agree with the way her partner handled the matter. But neither of the two seemed to be interested in who might have injured the young Hispanic.

One does not need to be a human rights activist to object to this type of conduct; common sense and decency are quite sufficient. When Cesar returned from the hospital, one week later he told me that the doctor treating him could not believe that the police called off his ambulance, but neither would I if I had not seen it with my own eyes. It was about one month later when Cesar's mother came around to inquire about her son. She had not seen him for weeks. When I realized that the top lock of his door was shut, I had a bad feeling in the pit of my stomach, since tenants were only able to lock that device from the inside. I opened the door with my master key and stepped back right away.

'Ay no, Dios mi Hijo! Una Ambulacia; llamense una Ambulancia!' The woman shouted coming running from the room. But it was too late for an ambulance by a long shot. Cesar Alvarez must have laid dead on his bed for days, with a big blood clot in his head. It was an hour later when the coroner carried Cesar's bodily remains off to the morgue. Right along with him went his dreams for a better life in the USA.

Springtime had once more come around to southern California. Although the surroundings were not adorned with as many blossoms as in Europe and most of the trees were not native to the area. The barren brownish hills surrounding the landscape, bordering on Mexico had received their usual, friendly greenish layer. The rainy season was over and the land was readying itself for another hot, dry summer.

A gentleman by the name of George Holst arrived as a new tenant at the Toreador. He was a certified electro technician and about to open a little TV repair shop in one of the motel rooms. The sociable Anglo American from Massachusetts was around fifty years old and affected by a walking impairment. As I passed by, he was busy exchanging the starter on his almost ancient automobile. In consideration of his disability I was somewhat concerned and asked, 'Are you coming clear down there?'

'Oh yes,' he replied, 'on the floor I am about as agile as any reptile. But you wouldn't happen to have a half inch ratchet I could borrow for an hour, would you?'

'Coming right up,' I hurried off to locate the tool. When he was done, he came back with a couple of small beer bottles in his hand. The two of us sat down and started a spontaneous conversation. George told me that he served in the military for a long time, including overseas. 'Mostly I worked on naval electronics, usually on sonars and radars.'

'And now you are fixing TVs?'

'Yes. I barely make enough to stay alive, but I am not unhappy. When you are poor you just need to be smart and frugal. Poverty requires a lot of self discipline. You must limit yourself to the bare necessities and buy only what you need, as well as know when and where to buy it. I usually purchase whatever is on sale, asides from that, I buy at outlet stores as well as second hand shops.' George gave me a couple of tips regarding various discount retailers in the vicinity. I appreciated his input since pinching pennies had long become a necessary habit for me as well.

The parking lot on the southern Toreador property was rented to a used car dealer and a night watchman seemed obligatory for this type of commerce in the area. Quite often in the evening I would meet the Mexican gentleman in charge of keeping an eye on the vehicles. Usually a fast crowd was gathering for a chat in the driveway of the establishment and I was almost proud to participate. Only Spanish was spoken and that gave me the opportunity to test my moderate skills in this language. The nature of the conversations was never complex; everyday struggles, family, the job and women were the usual topics. Occasionally a good looking young lady around twenty years old joined us. 'You speak Spanish?' she asked me somewhat surprised as she kept looking at me.

'And you fluent English!' I countered.

'Of course I do; I was born and raised here in San Alberto, my Mother is from Mexico, my father is American Native.' I gradually developed a fondness for the friendly, attractive Latina by the name of Sylvia. What I did not know at the time was that Sylvia was suffering from chemical dependency. Despite that aspect, the two of us became good friends, but I was about to learn that drug dependency happens to be an ailment exceptionally difficult to treat.

Again, I felt tense and nervous the morning I had to appear before the grand jury. I had not slept well the night before. Many hours I had spent trying to estimate my chances for obtaining help from that government agency. Although the offenses were numerous, the motives obvious, and the effects apparent, the self protective mechanism of the US system must not be underestimated. On the other hand, grand juries were specifically created to combat corruption within the system, but would they do so on behalf of an alien?

My guess was a chance of approximately fifty to fifty. With this figure in my mind, I entered the grand jury offices that morning.

'Unfortunately we have not been able to find a criminal conspiracy in your case, which does not mean that there could not be a conspiracy.' Mr. Bolt opened his speech. These words were already pointing in an unmistakable direction and, I suppose, the question why he hadn't looked more closely, he would have justified one way or the other. 'Why then was a series of burglaries against our business hushed up by police?' I pressed my point.

'Well, we concluded that Mr. Bricklin repossessed the computer because Mr. Sullivan owed Bricklin some money.' I was nothing short of perplexed about this pathetic objection.

'I am sorry sir, does the law of this country permit the commission of burglaries against a business under the pretext, that a staff member of the enterprise burglarized owes the burglar money?'

For a moment it seemed as if I had cornered Mr. Bolt with a sound argument. Almost embarrassed he replied with his head bowed downward, 'No it does not.' But he quickly recovered from my pointed reply and continued with increasing aggressiveness. 'The loss of that computer was not responsible for the bankruptcy of your business!'

'I never claimed it was, my complaint to the grand jury is based upon an entire series of criminal offenses, which remained uninvestigated and unprosecuted; the theft of the computer is only one aspect of it.'

'No, no,' Bolt returned almost helplessly, 'your entering this joint venture with Gale Cassell was sheer insanity; his equipment was nothing more than junk!'

'Those trucks were one to two years old top brand American commercial vehicles, sir!' I replied astounded, slowly shaking my head. 'And your CPA does not appear to be involved in this affair as you might think!' he continued.

'If so, where is our audit, where are the records he took and never returned to us?' Bolt did not answer this ques-

116

tion, but continued talking. 'This computer never really worked properly, you were just made to believe that it contained a list of your customers!'

'I know for a fact, that this computer contained much more than merely a customer list, sir.' Bolt seemed increasingly helpless, but continued with ridiculous objections. 'All the people we talked to asked how you were doing, except for this Sullivan!'

'Sullivan knows how I am doing; he does not need to ask, sir.'

'No, no, this Sullivan is a high roller with a big car and cigar!' Bolt was apparently running out of arguments to lead the conversation. To make matters worse he repeated the last sentence; obviously to prevent any discussion over relevant issues. In response to my question why we were refused burglary reports Mrs. James replied, 'It has never been established that these were true burglaries.' I believe her last words to me were, 'Are you married?' It would have been about as relevant as asking whether I had dandruff.

A slender elderly gentleman who watched this entire spectacle escorted me to the door. 'I will most likely be with the next grand jury, taking over in the new year. Maybe we will be able to help you some more on this.'

'Thank you,' I returned before leaving the offices. I appreciated his empathy, but I had my doubts. Mr. Bolt and Mrs. James were not the problem. Only very influential and powerful people within the US system were able to interrupt grand jury investigations.

'Somebody whistled them back!' was Tom's assessment of my latest fiasco with the American system and Sam shook his head in disbelief over the disappointing outcome of my efforts. It was only a few days thereafter when John Sullivan called me. 'You obviously made an attempt to gain some insight into our affair; what was the outcome?'

'You're supposed to be a high roller with a big car and a cigar, our venture with Cassell was allegedly sheer insanity because his vehicles were junk, and Bricklin stole the computer because you owed him money.' After I received only silence as a response, I asked 'are you still on the line?'

'Yes I'm here,' John answered.

'Do you still have the payroll slips to prove that Bricklin was paid fair and square?' I wanted to know. 'My God, if we prove that, the system will just come up with some other pretext to turn us away. I am afraid I do not even want to know who is behind all this!'

In the following months the Toreador was sold to a businessman from the Middle East. Rafael went into retirement and I had to return as a regular tenant into one of the motel rooms. One day I woke up in the middle of the night with excruciating pain in my lower back. As if I did not have enough health problems already, I started to develop kidney stones. Since I had not had medical care insurance for almost a decade and had not seen a doctor's practice or hospital from the inside in all these years, it was only a matter of time until something would go wrong. My friends brought me medications from Mexico, where drug preparations were less expensive and usually available without prescription, however that was no substitute for a physical examination by a physician. I had fixed my teeth with clove oil and zinc oxide as an American dental technician taught me. It seemed as if my life consisted of nothing but improvisations for years, and obviously for years to come.

One day Sylvia called me with a sobbing voice from the women's county jail. Apparently she had been on a nightly stroll with a friend of hers who apparently attempted to break in to a parked automobile. Sylvia did not even touch the vehicle at issue, but she was charged with co-accessory in an attempted burglary. The owner of the car did not want to press charges, but the police decided to prosecute the matter anyhow. If the state should lock up a twenty year old woman for three month over a trifle may be debatable. What really amazed me in this case was this 'as the mood takes you' approach to justice. In this instance the enthusiasm of the system to prosecute essentially nothing, but in my case be willing to sweep a hefty series of crimes under the carpet. But Sylvia as a Latina and I as a foreigner would hardly find much readiness from the government to protect our rights. Yet as perpetrators of an offense, the both of us would likely get to feel the merciless power of those enforcing the law. Justice and law enforcement in this country differed quite a bit from its counterparts in Western Europe. This was illustrated by various incidents making their rounds in the American media.

An inordinately high incident rate of prison suicides was under investigation. Numerous inmates allegedly hung themselves, but their feet were still standing on the floor when their corpses were found. In another state an official forensic institute found itself under the scrutiny of inquiries. The lab appeared to have been altering the results of their scientific work for years. Worse yet, this seemed to have been done on the behalf of the prosecutor. A worried judge commented: 'If the prosecution wanted proof, that somebody got killed by Martian rays, the institute delivered according evidence!' as it turned out there were even death sentences handed down based upon such manipulations.

In San Alberto the daughter of an investigator for the D.A.'s office stood before the court. The eighteen year old woman was obviously driving under the influence of alcohol. She provoked an accident with one fatality and one more person being injured. The young lady found a very merciful judge. She was sentenced to a jail term of one year. Approximately three months after the verdict, the widow of the deceased accident victim spotted the convicted drunk driver shopping in a department store. The female convict had been released from the penitentiary after serving merely one quarter of her sentence.

Around the same time another eighteen year old daughter from another family who had also provoked an accident while drunk driving within San Alberto County, had the same horrific outcome: one person killed, one injured. But this teenager was less fortunate in regard to her punishment; she received a hefty fifteen years in prison. The difference between those two sentences clearly illustrates the almost unlimited leeway for American judges in their powers of discretion, regarding the individual assessment of punishment.

A lasting experience of US justice came upon a waiter on his way home from work. In the evening hours he was stopped by police in his vehicle south of San Alberto, because one of his car taillights was not working properly. After the officer ordered the young man to fix the problem, the constable received the order to arrest the driver on the spot. Clueless about the reason for his incarceration the man was brought before the examining magistrate the subsequent morning. He was apparently suspected of having committed a robbery in a US state over one thousand kilometres away. After being told the date and time the offense at issue had been committed, the accused must have been confident of being released soon, since that very day and hour he was working at his current place of employment and numerous witnesses could testify to that. And they did. Nevertheless the accused was extradited to the state, which issued the warrant for his arrest and sentenced to ten years in prison. However, his employer kept fighting relentlessly for his wrongfully imprisoned employee. In the course of these efforts the restaurant owner was granted an audience at the offices of a federal senator. This mighty politician ordered the FBI to investigate this case at once, which quickly led to the apprehension of the real perpetrator. The poor waiter was released from prison and returned to his previous place of employment.

In numerous regions of the USA, law enforcement has seemed to go astray. Among the obvious leisure activities of a policeman in San Alberto were robberies, rape and shootings. He went to prison for many years. A deputy sheriff from the region appeared to maintain similar hobbies. According to the media, he wore women stockings over his face when he attempted to rob an elderly lady in her house. He doused the woman with lighter fluid and threatened to set her on fire if she would not give him money. An observant neighbour called the police and the robber was shot dead by a colleague. During the subsequent days, cocaine filled syringes were found strewn in the garden of the robbery victim's home.

Another young woman was directed to drive in a forested area near San Alberto, where she was raped and strangled by a policeman. A similar case was published roughly ten years ago in south-eastern California. In another state a federal officer shot an illegal border crosser in the back. Thereafter he dragged the dying man across the border into Mexico, where he left him to perish in the desert. A corporate executive sustained serious injuries when he got shot inside his villa after law enforcement officers broke into his home with storm trooper tactics. The police had obviously followed a tip off from an informer, claiming the stately building was a stash house for illegal drugs, but no drugs were found. A similar incident north of San Alberto County ended even worse. A large farm became the target of a nightly brake-in and hold-up by law enforcement. The farmer was shot dead. In this case the authorities were also after illegal drugs, but unable to find as much as the butt of a joint.

A particularly sad event occurred northwest of San Alberto. A teenager called police about his mother suffering from a nervous break down. The constables responded, broke into the locked room where the lady was hiding and shot the mother dead right in front of her adolescent son. An Escondera police officer fired off his pump gun during a hostage incident, but killed the hostage instead of the hostage taker. Two police officers on bicycles spotted a man with a pistol in his hand in downtown San Alberto. After that person did not respond to the shouting of the officers, they opened fire and emptied the clips of their pistols. The civilian with the gun remained unscathed, but the officers shot a hole in their own bicycle tire. Unfortunately, an innocent passer by also got hit by a police bullet and died as a consequence. A lawyer suffering from mental derangement, holding a pair of scissors and a baseball bat, was obviously damaging parked cars on a street in San Alberto. He was shot dead by police who, according to the media, handcuffed his corpse afterwards. An unarmed British citizen was also shot dead behind the steering wheel of his parked automobile. The deceased was obviously involved in a custody battle over his children with his divorced US wife.

In various counties of other states the FBI needed to step in and arrest several sheriffs, suspected of being involved in large scale drug dealings, blackmail and homicides. These obviously were not merely sheriffs' deputies, but sheriffs themselves, being the highest ranking law enforcement officers of an entire county. Deputy Sheriffs were arrested by the dozens in yet another state by federal authorities, and charged with corruption. Whatever measures currently being implemented to remove black sheep and incompetent personnel from law enforcement, before they become a serious problem and to keep them off police forces for good is proving insufficient.

In the meantime a piece of world history was being written. The communist eastern bloc had finally collapsed. Some people claimed it happened under the continuous pressure of the USA. Others just seemed to be glad that an oppressive regime finally met its end. The communist menace motivated Western Europe towards a decisive pro American attitude after the Second World War and that was a logical consequence. After all, the United States helped to end that war and subsequently built its military bases in various regions of Europe to keep the communists at bay. Europe was grateful for America's help. Undoubtedly the USA was considering the Nazis and, even more so, the Communists as a threat to the safety of their own country and the US engagement in Europe must have been based upon these strategic reasons. The obvious benefits of those US activities for Europeans could have been nothing but by-products of strictly national interests for the United States. Nonetheless, in order to operate their facilities in our continent effectively, America needed the goodwill of Europe's population. So the USA showed their best side and maintained the gloss of its self portraits as long as necessary.

Later, communism had lost its fangs and claws, but Western Europe had lost its status as an anti-communist bulwark for the USA. My home continent changed over night from a US protégée to an expendable and negligible global competitor for America. After the United States of America successfully fought political extremism to provide stability in Europe after the Second World War, the same country might henceforth secretly support Europe's political radicals, in order to achieve the very opposite. On the other hand, traditional inhabitants of post-communist countries are inclined to embrace pro-Americanism and where pro-Americanism might lead, I just had to learn the hard way.

After Rafael had left the Toreador for good, he realized that it was not yet time for his retirement. He took over the management of a small motel in San Martino. He offered me a similar position there and I was glad to find a new part time job, helping out a few hours a day, to earn some bread and egg money. I also became acquainted with Vicente, the manager of a used car lot adjacent to that motel. Whenever I called more than one old car my own, I left it at Vicente's lot for him to make a couple of dollars. And when I was without any transportation, Vicente left me one of his vehicles to get around town. Times were hard and money was scarce in those days. Vicente's financial situation resembled my own. An economic downturn seemed to have a grip on most areas in this nation. In several regions of San Alberto, where uncountable people used to make a living not long ago, locked doors and boarded up windows lined the streets. Even a number of large supermarkets were shutting down.

Sam who just returned from a trip to the Midwest informed me of similar developments in that region. This recession had not come around by total surprise. Saturation of the consumer market became obvious a couple of years ago. Consequently it was decided to stimulate the market by means of lower monthly payments for consumer items, but extending the payoff schedule over a longer period of time. In a society where almost everything is bought on credit, people are inclined to go out and spend money they don't even have. As a result, innumerable customers went into default, and the market value of their meanwhile used articles was far below the amount still owed to the business. Upon repossession of those products, dealers, brokers and financial institutions were facing tremendous losses and innumerable businesses nationwide, among them many new car dealers, went bankrupt, one after another. The ailing economy also took its toll upon the American people. Homeowners got kicked out of their houses and needed to move into rented apartments. A number of apartment dwellers were forced into miserly, little rented rooms and those unable to afford the latter joined the growing number of homeless roaming the city streets, sleeping under bridges and other structures where they found some protection from nature's elements.

This rapidly growing segment of that population was no longer made up of mostly mentally ill, alcoholics and drug dependents. Innumerable recently arrived participants in the world of the so-called 'bums' used to have a nice home and a decent job not long ago. America's hire today and fire tomorrow policies within private industries and commerce provided little, if any, livelihood security for their people. Powerful labour unions might sometimes negotiate right out exorbitant wages for their members, but unions can only protect workers, they cannot create jobs. Not every company maintained contracts with these syndicates and their marching into a small business may in some cases lead to its bankruptcy and therewith the loss of employment.

Job applicants in the USA needed to be prepared to answer questions about the colour of their bowel movements and their belief in only one God. Many employers demanded that their workers submitted to urine tests as a means to check for illegal substances. In at least one case, a lady was fired from her employ because the test revealed nicotine, of which her employer disapproved. Unemployment benefits are usually paid to those losing their job, but often for only a few months. The welfare systems of the individual states support primarily poor families with dependent children. The federal disability and social security institution provides financial subsidies to those chronically ill or disabled, as well as to senior citizens.

Poor folks were being met with almost fear and aversion in this society. This may be due to the fact that poverty is an inordinately high risk for the majority of the entire population. America tends to ignore poverty and is therefore not inclined to provide for those affected, beyond bare necessity, if even that. The tacit mind-set was that poverty should not exist, so let's pretend it simply doesn't. In a suburb of San Alberto signs were posted by an official authority prohibiting everybody from offering nourishment to indigent persons. In a neighbouring community a religious group vigorously fought against a free breakfast provided by the state for children of poor families. Their objection was based upon the prerogative that feeding children was solely the obligation of their parents. In summary, I kept discovering an America that appeared to be very reluctant to make adequate provisions for stability in the lives of its inhabitants.

In those days I had my last contact with Fred Steiger, our former dispatcher. He advised me about his coming under the scrutiny of fiscal government authorities. Based upon the conditions our company was being subjected to, we were very obviously unable to comply with all our obligations, including the internal revenue service. But as it seems, the same system, largely responsible for our incredible situation, was quasi presenting us with the bill for wrecking our livelihood. This was really rich!

CHAPTER EIGHT

One day all the tenants of the Toreador got their notice to leave. The buildings containing the motel rooms, as well as the apartment complex, were to be torn down. The historical commission was only able to save the main building from the wrecking ball. Over fifty people had to find a new place to live and I happened to be one of them. George Holst was fortunate to find a new location rather quickly. It was a shop in a commercial area only a couple of miles up the road. 'The place is not really meant for housing,' he commented, 'but I am about to install a bath tub, for washing parts of course,' he smirked. 'There is a small room, about six by eight feet that I do not really need.' George continued, 'I am looking for a subtenant.'

'How much you want for it?' I asked

'One hundred fifty dollars I suppose. I could use some help with the rent.'

'May I take a look at it?' I replied.

'Sure, come along.' I examined what I supposed was to become my new home.

'Beat's living in the back of a car,' I concluded and returned to the Toreador to gather my belongings. The two of us had found a new place to live. We celebrated our avoidance of homelessness with a big pizza. I suppose most Europeans would only shake their head over a festivity of indigence, but I had observed dozens of people in and around San Alberto residing in wooden boxes, hardly bigger than a coffin. A roof over ones head was not a matter of course in America.

George was an exceptionally forthcoming person with a big enough heart for almost everybody, but he also had an appreciable habit of not sticking his nose into other people's private affairs. Personally he must have wondered about my unusual situation during the past year. Over our last glass of wine, I decided to divulge the course my life took in the USA during the past ten years. George was not a man to show his emotions, but his pensive silence after I concluded my little narration was plenty of proof of his surprise over my story. 'Have you ever taken into consideration that this Cassell could be a regular informer of our federal government? If he is involved in numerous big scale sham operations, together with organized crime, he probably knows a lot about what is going on in these circles. His information about these activities could be very valuable to our system, which might protect him as long he keeps snitching on other crooks all around the country. Consequently you'll run against concrete walls to hold him accountable, as long as you aint got a diplomat or high ranking politician at your side.'

Now it was my turn to show a pensive expression on my face and to respond with silence for a short while. 'It almost seems that the government and the mafia are becoming increasingly hard to differentiate within this Machiavellian empire,' I said cynically, but as I spoke that very sentence I came to realize that my choice of words could hurt George's feelings. He appeared to be like John Sullivan, a critical patriot. I expected a reprimand, but George began to close his eyes, until only a slit of his irises remained visible. Then a typical sarcastic grin appeared on his face, 'Our justice system is a joke, you only need to learn how to laugh about it.'

As I was barely managing to stay alive, buying and selling used cars, George was busy all day long with his volt ohm meter, solder iron and oscilloscope, fixing the home electronics of his customers. He read numerous books of various contents until late at night that he had borrowed from the public library. He did not enjoy a happy life. His economic situation was marked by privation and his impairment forced him to use a walking cane, sometimes a crutch, but he never complained about it. 'That's life,' was his assessment of every situation that confronted him. Often on Saturday evenings a smile would appear on his face and he would announce, 'I have to go and drink beer.' He usually met with friends across the border until the following morning. It never ceased to amaze me how he got back in one piece. Now and then he needed to exit his automobile at the passenger side after returning, since his car's left door sustained some damage. 'Mexicans are wonderful people!' he stated, 'but they just can't drive!' He inspected the body damage on his vehicle as he peered through his spectacles, fixed with green electrical tape, with the facial expression of an insulted basset hound.

George just never seemed to get used to the traffic circles across the border. Much less did he ever develop a fondness for traffic lights, 'I just don't like a light bulb telling me what to do! – I never cared for other people's rules, I make my own.' Overall he was a special personality and he had become one of my best friends that I'd made in America. George was a born and raised American of Irish descent, who was apparently very intelligent but somewhat eccentric and unconventional. He used to live in Asia as well as in Europe for quite some time and he was not all that convinced about the claimed supremacy of the American way of life. His countrymen were, according to him, too inclined to believe instead of thinking for themselves. Ignorant people he tolerated only as silent listeners. 'But if somebody tells me. "George you are telling a bunch of bogus!" Then – I love it.' he stated, 'providing he can prove it. Sometimes I tend to believe I know everything!' No, everything he did not know by a long shot, but an incredible lot for a poor man. Yet he did not quite get along with just anybody and had a tendency towards caustic cynicism.

I anticipated that he, in his striving for wisdom in life, had come to realize that wisdom does not rule the world and the wisest path leading to a better future for mankind always seemed to turn into a philosophical pile of rubble, right after implementation. As a consequence he learned to accept human imperfection as an innate element of our life, including his own, with a unique combination of humour and bitterness. 'I sometimes act like an idiot. It seems as if I need that now and then for my peace of mind,' he said with a smirk. 'As long as I am able to look back and laugh over my childish behaviour, then it isn't a problem at all. But if I one day can no longer see the humour in my self-parody, I know I'm in trouble. Life is a game,' he resolved earnestly. 'If somebody takes his role in life too seriously, he is no longer taken serious by others.'

American flags were flying in front of many stores along the streets of San Alberto. Banners right beneath those read: "Support our troops in the gulf!" The US invasion in Iraq had just begun. George, a former military lieutenant slowly shook his head. 'Our country is not being attacked, so why should I support our troops in the gulf, – to throw fire-bombs on Iraqi women and children perhaps?' I reckoned that the US system wanted to awaken patriotic feelings among its population, but America was not very enthused about sending their sons into another battle on the opposite side of the globe.

I had started my own offensive by writing to approximately one hundred judges, magistrates and judicial offices in San Albert County and beyond, asking for assistance in my case. The yield of the responses was meagre as usual:

Dear (Sir)

I am in receipt of your August, 23 transmittal, including a copy of the August 7 letter to the (San Alberto) County Grand Jury. I appreciate your concern about matters which you feel may have been mishandled. The Court has no authority over the conduct of Grand Jury proceedings. It is within the complete discretion of the Grand Jury to look into the matter if they wish to do so and contact you accordingly.

Otherwise, the problems evidenced in your letter to the Grand Jury are matters which are appropriately referred to prosecutorial agencies of the state or county in regard to any criminal misconduct. I note that you at one time filed a civil action for damages relating to the matter, which, of course is another avenue of relief. The Court has no role in initiating or investigating criminal or civil complaints. Our role is merely to hear and adjudicate civil and criminal matters after they are brought to our attention through the legal process of filing civil and criminal complaints. I can only suggest that you continue to pursue matters with the agencies available to assist you, or through your own counsel.

Yours very truly, A. J. Judge, Superior Court of California

Dear (Sir)

Justice T. has asked me to acknowledge receipt of your letter of July 22.

Unfortunately, Supreme Court Justices are precluded from rendering the type of assistance you are seeking. He is sorry that he is unable to help you.

Sincerely, D. B. Secretary, US Supreme Court

Dear (Sir)

This will acknowledge receipt of your letter of August 19, with its enclosures.

As a US District court Judge, I have no control over the actions of the (San Alberto) County Grand Jury at all.

If you feel that your civil rights under the United States Constitution have been violated, the proper avenue for you is to take your complaint to the United States Attorney's Office in this district.

Sincerely yours, L. N. Judge, U.S. District Court

Dear (Sir)

This will acknowledge receipt of your letter / complaint report dated July 28.

After thorough consideration and careful review of its contents, we have concluded that the matters referred to in your letter are not within the federal jurisdiction of this office.

Since the subject matter of your letter appears to relate to a civil case in which you were a party, we suggest that you direct your questions to your attorney for whatever action he or she deems advisable.

We are therefore returning for your future use the enclosures that accompanied your letter to this office.

Thank you for your inquiry. We regret we are unable to be of assistance to you.

Very truly yours, D. S. Assistant US Attorney

Dear (Sir)

Thank you very much for your letter.

It has been a long tradition and Congressional courtesy to refer correspondence from another state to one of the Senators from that state. This gives each member of Congress the opportunity to be of service to the constituents they directly serve.

For this reason, I am sure you understand why I am for-warding your correspondence to Senator A. C. from your state. It is my hope that the matter can be resolved to your satisfaction as soon as possible.

Again, I appreciate your taking the time to contact me.

E. K. US – Senator

Dear (Sir)

Returned unfiled is your material received November 16. As you may appreciate the Courts are limited by law to hearing and deciding cases and may not participate in such matters as you present. The Supreme Court of California is an appellate court responsible for reviewing and deciding cases that have been petitioned for review from the lower courts in California. It is not empowered to con-duct investigations such as the one your petition suggests.

Very truly yours, J. R. Assistant Clerk Administrator, Supreme Court of California

Dear (Sir)

This is in response to your letter of May 26 to the United States Department of State.

It is being returned to you because it does not appear that this matter falls within the purview of the Secretary of State or the United States Department of State.

However, if the Consul referred to in your letter has been unable to carry out the duties of his office in this case, he should notify the appropriate local authorities in his consular district, and his government should contact the U. S. department of State.

I hope this information is helpful to you,

T. F. Paralegal, US Department of State

Needless to say, that I sent a copy of the last mentioned correspondence to my consulate. It appeared that the diplomats of my country seemed to be breaking out in cold sweat over the thought of having to knock on the door of the US foreign ministry and ask a difficult question on my behalf. My elaborate efforts were not entirely in vain, so to speak. Two county marshals stood at the door of George's shop one afternoon, looking for me. Some judges appeared to have been annoyed by my correspondence. I was told to direct my efforts at 'something else'. The constitutionally guaranteed right to address the government for grievances may also amount to nothing but worthless ink on worthless paper. And the only place to find sympathy as a foreigner in the USA seemed to be in the dictionary: somewhere between "Shit" and "Syphilis".

Armando Castro must have arrived at the same conclusion. From what he told me he worked as a sailor on a large American fishing boat around ten years prior. According to his statements, the machinist left the winch, which hauled in the fishing nets, running on very high speed. Castro got hit and broke his arm. The captain, however, was not concerned about the injury of his crewman. Moreover, Castro, with one arm in a sling, was sent to perform duties in the engine room of the rocking ship, where several steel pipes fell down on him. Castro sustained substantial head injuries, but, so he told me, the sizeable naval vessel went about its business on the seas for weeks, without making arrangements to bring the injured man to shore. After his return, physicians diagnosed permanent impairment to Castro's health and earning capability.

'Were you ever offered any compensation for this incident?' I asked him.

'Yes, I got a verbal offer for a half million dollars,' he said.

'Why didn't you accept that, it sounds like an appropriate amount at that time for a partial disability?' I replied.

'It was,' Castro returned, 'but this was a verbal offer. I had talked to several foreign sailors who also got injured on US ships and sustained permanent impairments. Just like me, they were offered adequate compensation initially. Subsequently, agents of the insurance carriers approached them. The seamen were told to have little choice but to accept a much smaller amount than agreed upon, or they would not get anything at all. So under these circumstances I decided to take my case to the courts, where I got promptly nothing at all.'

'How could this have happened?' I asked.

'It happened because my lawyer did not have a chance against the attorneys of the insurance company.'

'Who was the insurance carrier?' I wanted to know. Castro's answer made me pensive; the enterprise he named was indeed a giant of his trade and capable of shaking out entire armies of top notch attorneys from their sleeves, the world over.

'How did your lawyer represent you in court?' I wanted to know.

'I don't know,' Castro replied 'I wasn't there.'

'You mean you did not even go to attend the proceedings?' I asked surprised.

'Of course I went to court, but I was arrested. Somebody spread the rumour that I carried a gun on me. Fact of the matter is that I do not even possess a firearm, but I was kept in custody for many hours. Finally I was told to sign a form in English that I could not quite decipher. Afterwards I came to realize that I had signed a statement claiming that I was mentally ill.'

'Have you ever tried to re-file your suit?'

'Yes, but it was denied, since I had 'admitted' to being crazy.'

'America, the beautiful…!' was all that came to my mind in response.

Around that time a remarkable incident in San Alberto made the regional headlines. According to the media, two officers of the San Alberto Police kept beating a local resident half to death, until the victim succeeded in grabbing one of the constable's firearms. One officer was shot dead and the other was seriously injured. Evidently the two policemen seemed to be cruising a neighbourhood populated by black people, looking for a Negro to beat up, until they found one. The surviving officer claimed that the beating victim made an illegal U-turn with his automobile prior to the incident. Eye witnesses stated that no U-turn or other traffic violation had been committed whatsoever.

Another incident north of San Alberto County involved a

tow truck driver who was shot by police while behind the steering wheel of his moving vehicle. In this instance the officer who fired the shots made the statement that the truck driver had been swerving towards some pedestrians. At the subsequent court procedure the judge allegedly remarked diplomatically: 'In this country we don't shoot people to prevent traffic accidents!'

A growing number of similar incidents were reported from various parts of the nation over the past ten years. George's explanation for these disturbing developments was relatively simple. 'If any region within this country is expanding and growing during an economic boom, it needs additional police personnel. But private commerce will also hire employees for top wages under those circumstances. So hardly anybody who can qualify for that job, wants to become a constable.' He explained further, 'Private recruiting businesses are often hired to look for applicants in our large military camps all across the nation. There they are after soldiers who've served their obligatory two years in service and do not want to stay on beyond. Soldiers are trained in man-to-man combat, they learn to obey orders and have experience in handling firearms. Many enlisted men want to return home after leaving the service; some might have a criminal record. Others don't know how to read and write properly and if they were to cautiously check the few left over for personal character deficiencies, then the recruiters might come back empty handed. So the reports for qualifications are glossed up and a new bunch of morally defective police rookies will hit the streets, causing further problems.'

He seemed as disgusted with the situation as I was. 'Back in the old days you had to be at least six feet tall to become a policeman. Subsequently it was determined that this rule constituted discrimination. So they hired all these little runts, afraid of their own shadow. They shoot first and ask questions later.'

'This police misconduct appears to be a very recent phenomenon in California,' I said.

'You mean when they were beating on pregnant women with police batons in a city up north some years ago?' George returned sarcastically. I was short of an answer so George continued. 'It's kind of a law of the west. If they don't like you, you are about to get it!' But it was no longer only the west. It appeared to me that America had slowly begun to lose control of its law enforcement and those meant to uphold the laws were increasingly scoffing at it. The system, it seemed, persisted and even tolerated living with this condition. Yet if the state no longer obeys its own laws, it can't expect its people to do so, which may, sooner or later, create a vicious circle.

Sylvia had meanwhile reached the age of twenty-two and despite efforts from her family and me; she did not seem ready to understand that she could not just do as she pleased. Possession of illegal narcotics, being under the influence of drugs and riding on public transportation without a valid ticket were the charges she got confronted with, over and over again. And it was the legitimate duty of the system to prosecute the rebellious teenager who had become a young woman in the meantime.

When I went downtown to attend her appearance in court, I had the opportunity to view several legal proceedings. I was amazed over the difference in professionalism and performance between attorneys in private practice and public defenders of the county. The latter seemed to make, at best, an occasional half hearted attempt to mitigate for their client. The former put on a precise, convincing and flamboyant summing up for their mandate. This discrepancy may be tolerable in cases of misdemeanour trials, but statistics prove that in homicide cases, defendants represented by public defenders more often face a guilty verdict than those with a private, experienced criminal defence lawyer at their side.

George advised me that public defenders in the region were not really meant to engage in a tooth and nail fight for their clients. Their job was primarily to be present in the courtroom as prescribed by the law. 'Sam told me that in some states in the Midwest, every lawyer in private practice must serve a few weeks of every given year as a public defender. This seems to be a better alternative to these attorneys than being full time employees of the county.' George smiled sceptically and in doing so he always let me know that he was about to come up with something to counter my argument. 'If you get a renowned criminal defence lawyer assigned to you, you might get away with murder,' George smiled, 'but if an inexperienced corporate law attorney gets your case to defend you in a capital crime trial, you might lose your life, guilty or not.'

Decades after its abolition, California reintroduced the death penalty. Robert H. was one of the first persons to be executed in the gas chamber again. This chamber was a little containment in a large room with seats or benches for relatives of murder victims to watch the killer die. According to the media, Robert H. had snuffed out the life of another person before he, years later, killed two teenage youngsters during a robbery. Since Robert H. had already spent ten years in a penitentiary, where he seemed to behave, the argument was raised to convert his sentence to life in prison, but the State of California decided that he must pay with his life. On the day of his execution Robert H. was brought into the gas chamber and put into the chair, but was then taken back to his prison cell, only to be led on his last walk again hours later. He finally perished in the toxic fumes of acid and cyanide, with relatives of his victims watching him taking his last breath. Personally I am glad for never having met Robert H. neither would I want to meet any of those who actually went to watch him die.

In the meantime seven years had passed since I lost my drivers license. I had learnt to keep an intense eye on the rear view mirror and look out for police vehicles. But my hopes to solve that little handicap were shattered. Henceforth, any applicants for a driver's license needed to be in possession of a valid government social security card. So I had to spend the rest of my time in this country without a driving permit.

Tom had meanwhile taken a bit of time off from his immigration business to contact one more lawyer to review my case, but once more without any result whatsoever. It must have been around the seventh time I'd spent my scarce funds on legal counsel to no avail. So far I must have contacted about three dozen attorneys, two dozen legal aid institutions, around one hundred politicians and roughly one hundred and fifty government offices, asides from various media. I had just written to the highest chamber of government in my home country and received a 'no' for an answer.

Bob Nellis' betting days were over since he had recently passed away and Rafael decided to go into retirement for good after he was diagnosed with diabetes. Sam was roaming around the Midwest again and Tom seemed quite successful with his consulting business. George hung in there repairing electronics, and I barely made it selling old cars. Occasionally I stayed at Vicente's car lot during the day, making a couple of bucks now and then.

One day George was waving a letter he just received in the mail. It was the termination for his rental contract of the shop. Well, this broom closet never was a place to get homesick about, although I shared the small quarters often with Sylvia, when she got kicked out of her parent's apartment and it was as close as I had to call home and in that sense a privilege.

CHAPTER NINE

Latinos were less reliant on yellow pages and newspaper advertisements. Mouth to mouth propaganda played the head role around here if anybody had something to sell or was looking for a buy. In the parking lot of the supermarket, serving in this respect as the village square, I got a couple of addresses for available inexpensive living quarters.

The four narrow one-story buildings stood in a row spanning about sixty meters. The structures looked somewhat like horse stables converted into apartments and maybe that's what they were. Their shabby appearance would have rather befitted the poor section of town across the border. The sizeable yard stretching about twenty five meters in width along the edifices was made up of sandy earth and any type of motion, on foot or per automobile, proved to be a real challenge, particularly during the rainy season when the grounds turned to mud. Behind the door with the slightly askew number seven, I found a place to live for my remaining time in this country. Inside there was no actual ceiling, but merely the roof painted like the walls in a yellowish olive green. Along the main supporting beam an electric line powered a naked light bulb, which hung over the centre of the humble dwelling. To the back, an old couch stood there as if it had been ordered eons ago and not picked up. On the right side of the entrance a sink and stove with gas range stood side by side, adjoined by a couple of chairs and a rickety table.

Immediately behind the door to the left, a brave old big

refrigerator from the sixties still provided its reliable service. Behind the fridge, a small passage-way, whose partition door must have given up the ghost a long time ago, led into the bedroom. That chamber measured around two by four meters. The latter was the width of the building. On the opposite side of the main room the pathway opened into a small chamber measuring about two by three meters. On its right side the bathroom was located, with a toilet and a shower. The interior walls were made of painted wooden boards, with wide cracks between their connections, the linoleum floor was partly breaking away and one of the small windows had been repaired with cardboard. Yet there were also positive aspects about the place. For instance there was no need to keep an aquarium, not so much because of the slightly leaking roof, but watching cockroaches crawling all over the place can also be a very soothing and relaxing experience.

These subtenants came in three sizes and even the most powerful insecticides could not exterminate them, as I had soon found out. A few days after extensive spraying, their descendants were eyeballing me from every crack and crevice anew. The monthly rent of two hundred dollars per month including utilities ranked far below the average price for housing in the region, so there was no reason to complain. These shacks belonged to a friendly elderly Hispanic couple who lived in a separate, small house on the street front of the property. Rafael had the kindness to lend me his pickup truck for my move, but my financial situation was such that I could not pay a helper to help me hoist some heavy items, so I had to do it on my own. During the unloading, I suddenly felt a numb, warm feeling in my lower back and in the following years I had come to realize that I had sustained a permanent impairment to my back.

Meanwhile Sam had returned from his travels around the Midwest and was again looking for a place to live and he was satisfied with the little chamber adjacent to the bathroom. Since I had nothing left but buying and selling used cars as a means of income, I appreciated his help with the rent. A consular secretary had announced his visit at my new home. Why not, I thought, it might be interesting for those people to see how the other half lived. The young, sociable official did not make any comments about the place I had to call home, but quickly suggested we go to a restaurant, where I got the benefit of a free supper. 'Just between you and me,' he said soberly, 'if I were consul general I might have reacted a little bit different in response to your case.' Unfortunately he did not occupy that position, so nothing changed for my circumstances and me, I still did not receive the remotest little bit of legal assistance or diplomatic intervention.

After another one of my pleas for help got turned down by a US Senator, Sam commented 'I just cannot believe it, how they are chasing you away like a dog.

I have honestly never observed this type of response from our system.'

'Would you be willing to write a response on my behalf to this politician? Maybe my English is still insufficient to make my point.'

'Your English is amazingly good for somebody who did not grow up with it. You make some spelling errors and your sentence structure is occasionally unconventional, but your reports and explanations are clearly understandable, your English is not the problem here! But I will be glad to prepare a response to this senator for you.' I hardly had any hopes that the choice of words of a US university graduate would make a difference for me and persuade a high ranking politician to take appropriate measures on my behalf. And I was right. But an answer I got nonetheless.

Dear (Sir)

Thank you for your letter regarding your problems as a (foreign) Treaty Investor.

As I indicated to you earlier, the Judiciary Committee does not get involved in individual cases. Unfortunately, after examining the facts, I believe that the Judiciary Committee cannot be of any further assistance to you regarding this particular matter.

Again, thank you for your letter.

> *Sincerely, J. B. US – Senator,*
> *Chairman Committee of the Judiciary*

Sam just shook his head without saying a word. 'Well, I reckon this Senator had at least the courtesy in telling me to get lost, – twice now,' I concluded sarcastically.

'I just don't know what to say,' Sam replied, 'I've never really had any problems with our government.'

'No wonder.' I countered, 'You are a born and raised Anglo US -American!'

'You could be right,' Sam replied, 'that aspect may be of

importance. Perhaps our nation does not protect foreign treaty investors adequately, and their home countries are reluctant to intervene in our federal government proceedings on their behalf. That makes them predestined prey for the underworld.'

'I understand that laws, rules and regulations cannot always account for all and every situation which might occur in life, but there are also moral and ethical responsibilities within a state; not just jurisprudential aspects. What I have been getting in terms of a reply for over a decade is, at best, a polite form of deliberate indifference.'

'You're absolutely right,' Sam concluded, 'but American morals and ethics are a very complex issue in itself. I've never had the opportunity to travel to Europe, but I've met many Europeans over here. There is a kind of wholesomeness about most Europeans, which is lacking in the vast majority of US Americans. We share identical cultural roots and both of our cultures are predominately Christian. We read the same Bible, but we seem to interpret it in a different way. Religion has always had an influence upon society and society has always had an influence upon religion.'

'So I've noticed,' I replied. 'In particular Christian kindness appears to be facing some considerable shortcomings over here!'

'America is essentially "Old – Testamentarian",' Sam continued, 'despite our respect for and worship of Jesus Christ; we believe that Jesus Christ is our personal saviour who died on the cross in Golgotha for all the sins of mankind. Many of us over here interpret this central aspect of our religion as whatever wrongdoing we commit, against whomever during our entire lifetime, has already been atoned for by the expiation of our Lord Jesus Christ. Consequently we believe that we do not owe anything to those we hurt by our wicked deeds: not an apology, nor remorse and much less remuneration. Most of us do not really worship Jesus Christ for the mercy and compassion he felt for mankind. 'We are not really merciful or compassionate at all, except maybe to our next of kin. Our admiration for Jesus Christ is manifestly based upon his having paid in advance for all our wrongdoing, providing us with a quasi-blank, signed cheque for being our evil, ugly little selves. In return for being – so to speak – pardoned at a flat rate for life, we humbly pay our respect to God and Jesus his son; but by no means to our fellow men. We essentially consider ourselves to be sinners, imperfect human beings who do wrong by nature. It is our belief that God made us imperfect, but still loves us for being exactly that. Innumerable of my countrymen, be they religious or not, interpret this philosophical aspect in a peculiar way; If I am a creep, it was God who created me as a creep so it is my God given right – if not destiny – to remain exactly that.'

I was somewhat puzzled by Sam's revelations of US religiosity. It occurred to me that I still had not yet discovered every aspect of the American soul. The more I paid attention to the details of this society, the greater the crevice seemed to become between the new and the old worlds. 'Here we may be less reluctant to commit wrongs against others, since we consider each other as profoundly imperfect, if not to say unworthy. You Europeans are also Christians as we are, but you are also humanists as well. Therefore you have a greater inhibition to hurt others; at least on an individual basis.' Same went on, 'Respect for others and for the world around us cannot solely be derived from religion or from the law. It has to come from within a person, and develop as a vital aspect of their culture, although ideological elements may definitely contribute to decency and compassion. I have heard that churches and religion in Europe are to some extent co-administrated by the state, which seems to provide for the religious needs of the public, and to guide those desires into pragmatic directions, which do not conflict with humanitarian/secular principles or the law. But here in America we tend to leave as much as possible to the free market. Our, principally, appreciable freedom of religion allows practically everybody to start a religious congregation even in the absence of a bona fide theological education; all you might need is a building permit to erect the church.'

I sighed, 'I've observed this itinerant preacher mentality over here on various occasions and it seems obvious that values are being promoted by these people, not necessarily pastoral by European definitions. It's an undeniable fact that innumerable Europeans fled to the Americas to escape religious persecution in their home countries many years ago. Here they were allowed to practice their beliefs freely, and they were quickly accepted as members of the US Society. This is one of those nice aspects of US history known to Europeans. However, meanwhile Europe has become far more liberal regarding religious practices. But in our countries religion is still a rather private matter. People do not flaunt their beliefs all over the place,' I added. 'We've also succeeded in banning the ancient – and often frightening – powers of the clergy behind the church walls, where they belong. Churches and religious organizations seem to have much more influence upon daily life in the USA than in Europe these days.'

'In other words European religion is a part of your environment and society and, to a small extent, your state system, but it is not a quasi mandatory, central aspect of life.'

'I suppose that is the main distinction,' I concluded. 'Although there might be one or the other militant religionist, or even a hypocrite hiding behind his bible, most Europeans who believe in God are straight laced, decent, honest folk with an appropriate social conscience, which is an integral part of both, religion and society. Here in America it seems to be almost the opposite.'

'We've unfortunately been experiencing some abuse of our social systems for decades,' Sam informed me. 'This deplorable aspect of our society is being continuously emphasized by our ultra conservative politicians, who propose to abolish social benefits for almost everybody. Many Americans believe that welfare should not be a right, but a privilege to be provided for voluntarily, on a local basis. Some of us seem to envision a world where the needy may be treated like cattle or pets.'

'That is pretty scary indeed.' I must have been looking at Sam as if he was exaggerating. 'This is definitely capitalism,' Sam continued. 'It is almost anarchic capitalism. If you are sick, buy a hospital; if you like to go hiking, buy a mountain, if you want rights, buy a law firm. If you can't – then tough luck. Some people here in America would like to sell us the air to breathe!'

'What you are describing is a quasi- cannibalism' I returned, 'or a very degenerate form of capitalism to say the least. Capitalism needs a broad, open lane to move freely, efficiently and profitably, but with solid guardrails on each side and not just symbolic strings. Life sustaining wages, social security, a state of rights and ample personal freedom are essential for a healthy free market. These principles are not only based upon social conscience, but upon common sense.'

'Harry, you are drifting towards the middle as you often do.' Sam grinned. I smiled back as I said, 'I am, always have been, and always will be a political centrist. I like pragmatism. Any form of radicalism, particularly in politics keeps leading to privation for the public.'

'Wasn't it radical what you experienced when you had your business over here?' Sam countered my comment. 'Yes Sam, it was. But to me the USA is not a personification of capitalism, rather a notable, bad example of a corrupted form of capitalism,' I asserted. 'US capitalism seems unfortunately only one aspect of this nation which has gone astray. Nowadays this country may no longer be considered a state of rights by European definitions, if not to say by objective definitions. And many US citizens are not really what Europeans would perceive to be nice people.

'In all my years over here I eventually arrived at the conclusion that Europeans define decent people by fundamentally different standards. Here this qualification is obviously determined based upon somebody's regular Sunday church visits, not using expletive language and washing their hands after leaving the rest room. These appreciable distinctions are considered pleasant in my home continent, but such characteristics on their own would never be sufficient to constitute a decent human being.'

'We Americans are essentially otherworldly," Sam explained. 'We believe that this life on earth is only temporary, and our comportment towards the world and mankind are not of greatest importance. Most of us are convinced that another life in heaven is awaiting us, in a setting of streets paved with gold. This world here is not the centre of our existence. Honesty, respect, fairness and decency do not hold the same priority status, as they seem to have among Europeans. For these reasons we've become increasingly indifferent about treating humanity with the respect it deserves, and our continuing to do so will eventually drive us into political isolation. This is essentially a neo feudalistic first world country with third world values.'

'It seemed to us Europeans as if you had some progressive movements here in this country, like for instance the hippies.' Sam chuckled as he shook his head.

'Hippies were neither progressive nor a movement. They were the sons of America who did not want to be drafted into the military and subsequently die in Vietnam, and American daughters who shared those beliefs. Most of them did not really care about any Vietnamese losing their lives over there; they were merely concerned about not losing their own. Hippies were at best illustrious establishmentarians, believing in rights and duties; rights for themselves and duties for everybody else. Flowers and peace symbols are not necessarily indicators of progress. Our often cited sexual revolution also never really happened. We are a strictly monogamous oriented society, and many Americans still consider their wife as some type of chattel. And you may find some establishments where pornographic material is sold. But you go looking for an aesthetic, sensual nude picture of a beautiful woman in those places, then you will find mostly depictions of gynaecological details. Sensuality is kind of a taboo in our country, but all these 'down and dirty' graphics are somewhat tolerated. We are just a peculiar society.'

'Yes Sam, America is definitely a peculiar society. But for a foreigner like me these few obvious, cute little peculiarities are not the issue, but those we never get to hear about abroad. If the entire world population were aware where they really stood in today's America, most of them would not even want to set foot upon US soil. Yet your home country still appears to be perceived as a place of justice and state of rights today, as it was presumed to be when I left for the USA fifteen years ago. If a nation is obviously run by a ruthless dictatorship, Nazis or Stalinists, the problematic nature of a totalitarian regime and the consequences associated therewith are obvious to anybody. For a foreigner to expect certainty of rights in a place like that and under such conditions would be absurd. But a mighty, imperial and increasingly ruthless superpower with an outward appearance of a democratic state of rights, equality and freedom is essentially a mirage, and therewith poses a true challenge for mankind to confront.'

'During the two world wars we were definitely better off over here, than in Europe,' Sam explained. 'But our legendary freedom was always to be understood in a rather geographical way. We Americans can travel around freely

154

in a big, beautiful land and we may settle or remain temporarily in our various regions and climatic zones wherever we please. But the golden rule still applies here, as it always has; the one with the gold makes the rules. How our justice system can malfunction, well you unfortunately had to find out the hard way. But I still must stress that situations don't always deteriorate here as you've experienced. Regrettably nobody knows when and where it might happen again or how often it's currently happening. People being subjected to substantial wrongdoing in this nation are probably not easily identifiable as a group. Black persons and foreigners seem to be frequently among them, as are Asians and Latinos. But it looks to me as if American Natives often receive the harshest treatment from our system. – Why? I don't really know. – Perhaps because our so called 'Indians' never adapted entirely to our ideals and our way of life.'

While Sam called his home country a first world nation with third world values, George made a somewhat more diplomatic analysis of the USA. 'We are actually a republic with democratic elements; we usually elect those who will appoint others.' Tom was however convinced about his homeland being a true democracy. 'But you are right,' he added, 'our justice system is unpredictable.'

Hardly any American would dare to call the USA judicial system corrupt, or its government crooked. Such caustic criticism is not permissible in a land where people are taught from early childhood onward that it's supposed to be the best place to live on the face of this earth. The US system only 'makes mistakes', but hardly anybody would want to establish a statistic, proving that the term 'mistakes' could be a mild understatement. In that respect I could only quote a comment George made not long ago, 'Over here, if you say the truth in the wrong place and at the wrong time, you might end up with a hole in your head!'

The obvious question of whether the overall civil rights situation for people in America had declined dramatically or just moderately during the past decade, I will never be able to answer. Everybody agreed that it has, indeed, gotten worse, but I was at the very time, when this liberal era came to its end, still in a phase of discovery and analysis in the USA, and unable to make a comparison. When I left Europe, our continent was still somewhat in a state of appreciation over America's intervention during the Second World War. It was our belief that this US engagement had been based primarily upon humanitarian motives. We obviously neglected to take a close look at our supposed saviours. But in light of the circumstances nobody wanted to. America was the good guys, the Nazis and the Communists were the bad guys. That was the simplicity of political prerogatives under which we were brought up and I just 'bought it', hook, line and sinker.

Meanwhile the statutes of limitations respective to criminal charges for my debts incurred in my country and lost in my American dream had run out. I was able to return home without the risk of ending up in a penitentiary for criminal conduct, committed by a foreign nation. But almost until my last day in this country I continued to ask official agencies in the USA for help. Since my return trip to Europe was scheduled, I left the address of my consulate as a reply address and a response arrived thereat.

Dear (Sir)

Thank you for your letter to Attorney General D. L.

We regret that we cannot be of help to you in this matter. The California Attorney General's authority is limited by law. He is only authorized to represent the State and state government officials. Legal actions presented to the courts are on behalf of the collective interests of the people in California.

The Attorney General is not funded nor authorized by the California Legislature to provide legal research, legal analysis, legal advice, or to represent private individuals under any circumstances.

If you need advice or representation, we suggest you consult a private attorney who could directly represent your interests. We regret that we could not be of further assistance to you, but hope that the information we have provided clarifies our restriction in regard to your request.

> **Sincerely, P. P. Department of Justice,**
> **State of California**

'Is this because you are a foreigner in this country?' The consul seemed to remark, rather than ask, in the face of these charming lines. I no longer remember my answer. 'The American system has totally failed in your case,' was yet another official assessment I received. In principle I could only agree, but I had expected a lot more support and intervention from the side of my home country under these circumstances. Yet a previous diplomatic remark, 'I suppose we could call on the U.S. Department of State in your matter, but whether that would be of any help is another question!' was an unambiguous hint that diplomats or perhaps even statesmen could be received with the same attitude of arrogance by the system of this nation, as I had experienced myself.

At that point in time I still had plenty of hopes that my deteriorated health could be treated, and all of my ailments cured, so I would be able to work again in the not too distant future. Unfortunately this self assessment turned out to be wishful thinking. Although I underwent several surgeries, a meagre existence as a recipient of a state disability pension was awaiting me. For the rest of my days I was to be dependent upon daily medications and permanently bereft of my earning capability. However, at the time I was unaware of all that I would have to deal with after my journey to my homeland was accomplished.

I was standing there above the grassy slope behind the South San Martino Boulevard and was looking down on what was left of the Toreador. Unattractive, cubical shaped commercial structures surrounded the good old main building of the former motel. The pool had been filled in and had become part of the parking lot. The stylish setting of this complex was my only US place of residence that I had grew fond of and it almost broke my heart looking at its remains. Maybe it was just time for it to go, as it was for me. This little border town had accommodated me for a total of fourteen years. Most of my time around this vicinity had been marked by privation and hardship, but the mostly Latino population of San Martino helped me to survive and get through a long and difficult period of my life. Looking back I almost felt embarrassed over my reluctance towards Latin Americans during my first years in America. I anticipated encountering rejection because of cultural differences. Subsequently I had to learn that Latin American culture might be different, but the mentality of these people was much closer to Europeans than Anglo Americans.

It was early in the morning, when Armando Castro brought me to the bus terminal in San Alberto. I was traveling light. One mid size and one small suitcase was all I had left after fifteen years in the USA. After the bus turned onto the freeway I kept looking out the window and realized how much the city had changed in all this time. Since my arrival in this town, over fifteen years ago, only the chamber of commerce building towered over the roofs of San Alberto. Now around a half dozen skyscrapers were reaching out to the heavens. The sun, as it seemed, timidly tried to penetrate the usual mist, covering the coastal region in the morning hours this time of the year and reflected its dim shine upon the glass fronts of the high rise structures. I let the scenery pass by without looking back.

Around forty minutes later the large vehicle stopped at the US border patrol checkpoint and a federal officer boarded the bus. Politely he asked every passenger for his citizenship. 'I'm an American citizen,' I responded to his question. The agent did not seem to doubt my practically accent free words, as he waved and nodded, before he left the vehicle through the back door. As a matter of fact, I almost felt as if I was an American after one and one half decades in this country. Less than five years of US residency would have been sufficient for me to apply for citizenship, but I no longer cared to call this nation mine.

The big airliner slowly gained height, as it cruised over Los Angeles. I had the opportunity to get one last look at the biggest city on the US west coast from a bird's perspective. Actually it was rather a giant village than a city. Hundreds of thousands of mostly one family homes stretched out over almost five hundred square miles of territory. It was an impressive sight, particularly at night.

Wistful but relieved at the same time, I was watching what used to be my homeland of choice slowly passing beneath me, from the Rockies over the Midwest to the dim and distant lights of the east coast. Then I returned back to the darkness I first came from, early that late summer morning eighteen years ago. I realized with some relief that my ill fated quest to the New World had come to an end at last. –